Kathleen Christensen

Women and Home-based Work

The Unspoken Contract

Henry Holt and Company   New York

Published by Henry Holt and Company, Inc.,
115 West 18th Street, New York, New York 10011.
Published in Canada by Fitzhenry & Whiteside Limited,
195 Allstate Parkway, Markham, Ontario L3R 4T8.

Library of Congress Cataloging-in-Publication Data
Christensen, K. (Kathleen)
Women and home-based work.
Bibliography: p.
1. Self-employed women—United States.   2. Home-based
businesses—United States.   3. Work and Family—
United States.   I. Title.
HD6072.6.U5C47   1987   305.4'3   87-8527
ISBN 0-8050-0386-X

First Edition

Designed by Kate Nichols
Printed in the United States of America
10 9 8 7 6 5 4 3 2 1

ISBN 0-8050-0386-X

To David Mann

Contents

Acknowledgments

I am particularly indebted to the 14,000 *Family Circle* readers who answered my survey and the one hundred women from around the United States who met with me to talk about their experiences working at home. I owe a special thanks to my colleagues and friends who offered insights and suggestions on the manuscript: Michael Brill; Kim Christensen; Tobi Dress; Faye Duchin; Abby Hamlin; Martin Krasney; David Mann; Michael Moskowitz; Nora Rubenstein; Barbara Katz Rothman; Susan Sternberg; James Wall; Judith Kubran and Richard Berk. Financial support for this research was provided by grants and contracts from the U.S. Department of Health and Human Services and the Office of Technology Assessment, U.S. Congress. Research assistance was given by Bonnie Scott, Gregg Van Ryzin, Rosalind Eichenstein, Tahire Erman, Nava Lerer, and Adrianne Royals. Harold Proshansky and Steven Cahn of the Graduate School, City University of New York, provided the intellectual and institutional climate necessary for me to write this book. Finally, I want to thank Nelson

Buhler, who brought this project to the attention of Henry Holt and Company, and David Stanford, my editor at Holt, who provided keen insights, as well as constant enthusiasm, on the project.

Kathleen Christensen
New York City
March 1987

Introduction

This is a book about women working at home. At first glance, nothing could be more commonplace. Women have always worked in their homes. As wives and mothers, we cook and clean, care for children, tend to husbands. We create havens for our loved ones, refuges from our foes. As vital as these labors are, they are not the stuff of which this book is made.

This is a book about women working *for pay* in their homes. These women are mothers and grandmothers, married and single, with children and without, the wildly successful and the painfully struggling. Some have skills that are in demand in the marketplace; others do not. Some are women with options who embrace the chance to work at home as the ideal way to attain their goals. Others are women of desperation who have few options and accept the home as the workplace of last resort. Between the women of options and the women of desperation are legions of women of circumstance. Working at home suits their purposes better than not working, but it is far from ideal.

The reality is that the contemporary American home has not been designed to accommodate work at home, much less to see the woman there as a wage earner. A woman at home is viewed first and foremost in her domestic roles as wife, mother, and homemaker. To introduce wage-earning work into the home requires that she re-educate her husband, children, friends, neighbors, as well as clients and supervisors, to the realities of working there.

That these realities remain invisible is no accident. The home is a private place and what goes on there is typically a private affair. Although work is inherently public, when taken into the home it literally is lost sight of, becoming hidden from public view. Yet, women who work at home do not want to hide. They want their stories told.

This was made clear by the thousands of women who were willing to talk to me candidly about the worlds in which they live and work. Over the course of two years, I have met women engaged in all sorts of work at home, including word processing, typing, data entry, as well as urban planning, accounting, market research, sewing, knitting, and child care. Some are just beginning their careers, others drawing them to a close; some work at home as a transitional stage in their children's lives; others pursue it as the desired goal. All are white, most middle-class—as is the group which responded to my survey. Although certainly not exhaustive in terms of all women who work at home, they are representative of national trends among home-based working women.

As I began to travel around the country in 1985, meeting with women who had responded to the survey, I quickly discovered that within this common culture of the middle class stand uncommon women, more dissimilar than similar to one another. Our language has led us to believe in the singularity of the American woman. We speak of the "working woman" as if she were only one. Nothing could be more false. There are career women, who have staked their lives on their work. There are women doing piecework, determined to eke out a living or to supplement their husbands' incomes. There are retired women, desperate to find a way to bolster a spare Social Security or pension check. There are women who want to re-enter the labor force after twenty years of child rearing, only to discover that their homemaking skills are deemed worthless by potential employers. Each working woman has her own work history. Being raised in the 1930s prepared a woman for wage-earning work quite differently from being raised in the 1950s. Women of all these circumstances, ages, and inclinations are now in the workplace and the workplace does not quite know what to do with them.

Although jobs have been created, slots filled, advancement opportunities opened up, the profound reality is that the workplace was designed over time not for women with family responsibilities, not for two-job households, not for women whose skills were honed running a home rather than a corporation. The workplace was designed and evolved over time for men who lived in two-parent households, in which the division of labor was quite clear: the private sphere of the home was the woman's responsibility; the public sphere of breadwinning was the man's. He could devote his energies to his job, knowing his wife would be home to cook, clean, chauffeur and coordinate. She could devote herself to running the household, knowing her husband would pay the mortgage, buy the food and provide for the necessities of their lives. That has largely changed as the economy has changed.

Most two-parent families now need two incomes in order to survive. As a result, nearly two-thirds of all mothers work for pay, a complete reversal from the situation in the 1950s, when nearly two-thirds stayed home without wage-earning work. Yet the division of labor within the home has not kept pace with changes in the workplace. Women continue to assume most if not all responsibilities for housework and child care.

Some women are content with this arrangement, others not; the difference in attitude depends on how they see themselves. Women who view their roles as wives and mothers as their primary ones may be reluctant to relinquish the moral authority traditionally accorded them. A woman who feels that the terms of these roles must be open to negotiation will assume some responsibilities, under some conditions, but may expect her husband or other members of the family to assume others. For her, the responsibilities are part of a negotiable social contract.

But not all working women have a partner. With a divorce rate of fifty percent, increasing numbers of women are thrust into being the sole support for themselves and their families. Some are prepared for this role, others are not.

It is within this changing context of women and work that home-based work must be viewed. Why a woman decides to work at home has everything to do with her history, with how she sees her roles, and with her options in the workplace. And the decision is not always easy.

For all of the advances women have made in the last twenty years, I think this is one of the cruelest of times. Women, much more than men in today's society, have to make a decision whether to love or to earn. Despite the cheerful optimism of many women's magazines, to choose one often precludes the other, and to choose both often proves impossible and self-defeating. In striking a bargain between work and family, many women are left exhausted, overextended, and feeling that they are not succeeding on either front. There is now a generation of women who, though mostly raised by women who stayed home, came of age expecting to work. And yet the role models for combining work and family are virtually nonexistent. Most jobs are simply not suited for women who have full responsibility at home in addition to the demands of their work.

For many women, home-based work seemed as though it would be the great panacea, the one option that would include all options. A woman could accomplish the success and autonomy denied her in the marketplace by starting her business at home. She could have it all, work and family, in the same place. For some the prophecy came true, but not for others. As the stories in the book reveal, many women who were attracted to the option and pursued it experienced disappointment. What should have been the ideal solution did not work. Some of the difficulty in working at home had to do with the conflict between the demands of the home environment and of the job. But a large measure of their pain came from the unspoken terms and expectations of their lives and marriages.

As I talked to these women, it became clear that their decisions to work at home, the ways in which they structured housework and child care, and the manner in which they handled employers or clients were all tied to the unspoken contracts of their lives—those implicit expectations they have about who they are and what they are supposed to do. To explore and successfully deal with home-based work forces one to understand the power and leverage of these unspoken contracts. It is toward that understanding that I have directed the focus of this book.

Women and Home-based Work

1

The Survey

The images are seductive. A computer programmer from California moves to the splendor of the Rocky Mountains and stays in contact with her Los Angeles office via computer. A manager starts her own consulting business, combining career and family obligations. A secretary stays home to care for her sick child; she hooks up her modem and does the office work between calls to the doctor.

Like all stereotypes, these images are limited reflections of reality. Yet they exercise a powerful hold over the public imagination. Home-based work, sometimes called "telecommuting" or "homework," has been actively promoted as the answer to many work-family conflicts of the 1980s.

Several years ago, due to a convergence of personal and professional interests, I decided to look behind the public images of home-based work. Based on initial conversations with women who had tried it, I was convinced that the realities would be more complicated than the images.

People have asked how I got involved in the research and why I decided to write this book. Like so many things that become important in one's life, my first encounters with the issues of home-based work were casual. However, as a professor of environmental psychology with a special concern with women's issues, I wondered whether the home environment could be successfully transformed into a professional environment and I had the opportunity to turn this questioning into a full-scale research project.

I first became aware of home-based work in the summer of 1983 when I read about a bill before Congress that would have offered tax incentives to families to buy home computers. One rationale for the bill (which was never passed) was that working at home would suit the needs of working mothers. At about the same time, a major business products company began running an ad that showed a woman happily working at her kitchen computer while her baby played quietly behind her. Although I did not have young children, it struck me as extremely unlikely that an infant would smilingly acquiesce to her mother working eight hours a day at a computer. But right or wrong, this ad expressed the growing expectation that computers would provide the way home for many workers.

The emphasis on computers was fueled in part by ideas presented in Alvin Toffler's 1980 book, *The Third Wave*. Toffler argued that as the structure of our economy changed from industrial to information-based, the computer would offer more freedom in the workplace, including the possibility of taking work home to the "electronic cottage." Another futurist at the time, Jack Nilles, coined the term "telecommuting."

As we were being drawn further and further into the electronic age, entrepreneurship was also increasingly gaining our attention. And the home was the perfect place for entrepreneurs: tax advantages, minimal capital needs, and low overhead would minimize risks. Dozens of books and magazine articles extolled the promise of home-based work for all types of people: discontented employees, mothers of young children, women who wanted to reenter the job market after raising their children, computer buffs, and loners. "During the recent baby boomlet," proclaimed *Newsweek* in January 1984, "many working mothers, and a few fathers, have discovered the fact that home-based jobs can be easier to balance with child care. Retirees and the disabled are seeking increasingly to supplement their benefits with paying tasks."

By the mid-1980s, the push for home-based work had begun. Economic and social forces had converged to create a positive image on several fronts. Women would earn money and raise their children in the same place at the same time; computers would allow millions of employees to avoid commuting to the office; and the home would shelter the efforts of the fledgling entrepreneur. According to these alluring images, working at home would provide a relatively effortless way to eliminate all sorts of problems from child care and office politics to commuting and the need for professional wardrobes. Workers could say good-bye to the office and head home with their computer. They could scan the want ads and find a company that would hire them to work at home. They could quit their jobs and start a little business on the side. Though the imagery was attractive, the glibness of the messages was unconvincing, particularly for women, and I became interested in finding out how the reality of home-based work compared to the fantasy.

In 1984, with funding from the U.S. Department of Health and Human Services and the Congressional Office of Technology Assessment, I began to talk to women in the New York area who worked in their homes. As a social scientist who often finds people reluctant to give interviews to a stranger, I was struck by the surprising willingness of these women to talk. Many expressed relief at finally being able to share their experiences. Despite all of the hype about the advantages of home-based work, when they actually tried it many had experienced loneliness, a lack of credibility, and, in some cases, a deep sense of failure. Feeling cut off and often frustrated, many were happy for the chance to "report back" on their experiences.

For many, my initial telephone call was the first time anyone had asked them about what it was like to work at home. Even the questionnaires in women's magazines had ignored them, asking, "Do you have a job outside the home?" and providing no box for them to check. In addition to not being taken seriously as wage earners, others found working at home to be a painfully solitary experience. They worked in neighborhoods that were often deserted, rarely knowing anyone else who tried to combine work and family in the same place. The isolation was compounded for some by a sense of failure bred by the recent spate of magazine articles and how-to books that had led them to believe it would all be so simple to work at home, take care of the baby at the same time, start a new business, and be a raving success. They felt under pressure since it was supposed to be so simple to succeed. And when they didn't, they considered themselves failures, often apologizing for painting such a bleak picture of what was supposed to be the perfect solution.

It was clear that there were many interesting stories to be told about home-based work. Since these women did not go to centralized work sites, rarely if ever belonged to unions, and at the time were not surveyed by the federal government's data collection agencies, I turned to a magazine survey as the best way to identify and locate women who worked in their homes.

I chose *Family Circle* as the most effective vehicle for my survey because it was read by roughly 19 million women, including homemakers as well as professional, managerial, and clerical working women.

Of the 14,000 women who responded, nearly 11,000 sent their names, addresses, and phone numbers, indicating that they would like to be interviewed in more detail about what it was like to work at home. Two thousand of the respondents sent letters describing their work and reasons for working at home, many including photographs of themselves and samples of their work. Hundreds more sent thank-you notes for the survey, many saying it was the first survey that had taken them seriously.

The survey results, as well as recently released data from the U.S. Bureau of Labor Statistics (BLS), can begin to provide insights into home-based workers. According to the BLS, five million men and four million women work eight or more hours per week at home as part of their primary (non-farm) jobs. The majority appear to be people who bring work home as overtime from their primary jobs. But 1.9 million Americans work exclusively at home, and about two-thirds of them are women; they average a twenty-seven-hour work week.

The survey responses provided important information to help put together a realistic picture of the lives of women who work exclusively at home. Of the 14,000 respondents, over 7,000 worked at home. Most were involved in clerical work (including typing, bookkeeping, insurance claims rating, and data entry work on computers); craftswork (such as sewing, knitting, and embroidery); and professional occupations (such as accounting, architecture, planning and writing). Despite the notion that companies were hiring large numbers of employees to work at home, we found that nearly four out of every five women were self-employed and worked alone for an average of twenty hours a week. The idea that computers are the central factor in the proliferation of home-based arrangements was also challenged: we found that only one in four clerical workers and one in three professionals used them.

Half of the women who worked at home were mothers who made their decisions based on family reasons. But in contrast to the ads showing women happily working with their children nearby, half of the professional and clerical women with young children relied on paid or unpaid child care so they could get their work done. Those who didn't have help said they often worked late into the night after their children were asleep.

The women without children worked at home primarily for work-related reasons: to work in their own way and at their own pace; to be more productive; or to save on overhead. Although most of the women reported advantages to home-based work, most also saw disadvantages in the situation. The two most frequently cited complaints were isolation and the fact that they didn't earn enough money. Working at home eliminates the boundary between work and family, so that the women often find they never can leave their work. The constant pressure of work is exacerbated by the sheer solitariness of the situation. These are women who are working alone at home, often cut off from any social network, who feel that they are not remunerated sufficiently for their efforts, often are not taken seriously, and sometimes can feel trapped by the combination of work and family in one place.

The preliminary findings of the survey certainly challenged many of the common images of home-based work. Yet the survey results told only the beginning of a very interesting story. Its details had to be told in the context of individual women's lives.

In 1985, I met with over one hundred women around the country to talk about their experiences of working at home. Each invited me to her home. All of them wanted people who didn't work at home to understand what it is really like. Many were also hungry for details of other women's experiences working at home. Often they knew no one else who was doing it.

The life stories of twenty of these women form the basis of this book. Most are married with young children, but some are empty nesters who view paying work in an entirely different fashion now that they have raised their families. Others are entirely on their own, having been divorced or never married.

As I talked to these women I became convinced that many of the public images of home-based work perpetuate a potentially harmful myth. Although home-based work can provide the perfect solution for some, it can be a calamity for others and simply difficult for most. Like any job option it has unique advantages and disadvantages. The idea that it is a relatively simple solution to complex work and family problems is a cruel illusion, implying that a woman will be able to resolve these problems by simply changing the place where she works. To embrace that assumption is to ignore the power of the unspoken contracts of our lives. It is in the understanding and alteration of these unspoken contracts, rather than in simply changing the location of the workplace, that a resolution of the conflicting demands of work and family will be found.

2

Homemakers Who Need to Earn Money

More mothers have paying jobs today than ever before, but combining work and family is no easy task, particularly when the children are young. For nearly 600,000 women with children under six, a home-based job has been their attempt at a solution. For many, working at home provides the closest alternative to being the full-time homemakers they wanted to be. The women in this chapter are traditional wives and mothers who think of themselves primarily as homemakers. All now have home-based jobs—occasionally out of choice, mostly out of financial need.

To protect the identities of people described in this book, all names have been changed as well as some of the details of their personal lives. All quotes, however, come directly from the interviews I've had with the women or their husbands.

Jennifer Beck

Jennifer is a woman who has been able to make choices all her life. She was born and raised in Seattle, Washington. The eldest of four

ne was brought up to believe that there was no difference
en boys' chores and girls' chores. She did them all—from
pping wood to mowing the lawn to sewing, cleaning, and cook-
g. "It made me feel like I could do anything I wanted, that I was
ot limited." Yet as a devout Mormon, she was dedicated to having
a family and being the kind of wife and mother she was brought up
to revere.

After high school, she attended a local college for two years but
quit when she married her high school boyfriend Daryl. Because
her primary goal was to be a good mother, Jennifer saw no need to
finish college nor to make specific plans for a wage-earning career.
Her career was to be at home; his was as the breadwinner. By the
time they married, Daryl had already started a construction company, capitalized through family loans, intending to earn enough to
support their family. Furthermore, he and Jennifer had a clear understanding about their priorities. When they married they made a
commitment to each other that once they had children they would
never put themselves in a financial situation that required Jennifer
to take a job.

Her views toward motherhood were unequivocal. "I decided that
I couldn't have kids and delegate that responsibility to someone
else. If I made the decision to have children, then it was my responsibility to raise them. You make a compromise when you delegate that authority to someone else."

It wasn't a compromise she was willing to make. In her mind she
would violate her most important obligation, which was to be the
moral authority for her children. According to Jennifer, a good
mother is not just the physical caretaker of the child but, more
important, is the child's moral teacher. "If I let someone else raise
my child, they would teach my child what words are good and bad
to say. They would teach my child what is acceptable and not. They
could teach them what is right and wrong. What they teach might
be different from what we believed. Then I would have to live with
my children as they were raised by someone else."

Raising her children meant being completely involved in their lives and being there even when they weren't aware and didn't care if she was around. Jennifer wanted to ensure that her children had the security and knowledge that she was always accessible. Being reliable and dependable as a mother was more important to her than pursuing a wage-earning career.

As an active member of her church Jennifer was surrounded by friends and family who shared her values. She could depend on them for both moral and social support when needed. In turn, she felt a strong commitment to her church and agreed early in her marriage to teach a daily seminary class to high school students. Jennifer's sense of herself as a woman, a wife, a mother, and home-maker were enhanced and strengthened by her community values. In a culture that has devalued the full-time homemaker Jennifer has maintained positive feelings about that job.

"I love to clean. I love to cook. I love to sew and I love to decorate things. I even love to do the grocery shopping—weird house-wifely kinds of things. It is really an art." In addition, she takes great pride in doing all of those things very well. "You can be either a frump or you can really be an all-out, knock-out, drag-out, walk-right-out-of-*Vogue* housewife. That's what I want to be."

And she is. At 5'10", with blonde hair and deep blue eyes she is strikingly pretty. She walks with the pronounced confidence of someone at peace with her life. An element of that peace is the clarity of her convictions and the ability to assert her needs as they arise and change over time. So although she and Daryl had structured their lives so they could live on his annual income, she decided shortly after the birth of their first daughter, in 1980, that she wanted a job.

"I am a very independent person and the thought of Daryl making all the money and me spending all the money kind of grated against my nerves. Also, I didn't want to be just a mom, because I am a person before anything else and I thought it was important that my children see me in a many-faceted way." She recognized that her job at home as wife and mother was full-time, but she wanted to keep some of her own identity through a paying job.

She had been sewing since she was a teenager and decided to start a home-based sewing business. "I was basically lucky. I had a talent that was marketable and that I could do from home."

Daryl understood her desire to work but also agreed it should be at home. "He and I came up with the idea of me working at home, it wasn't like I had to sell him on it. He was open to it. His only concern was whether I could handle it."

Her priorities were clear from the start. "Work is real important to me as an outlet, but it will never be the number one thing in my life. My family will always come first and I will never put work before it."

The couple had their second child in 1982 and their third in late 1983. By the time Jennifer was 26, she had three children under the age of 5 and was working 25 to 30 hours a week sewing for clients. Since the family has never needed her income, they have a different attitude toward her money.

"My money is my money—it's the fun money. His money is boring—it pays the bills. My money pays for us to go out on Friday nights or take the kids to the zoo or to McDonald's." Although they keep their money in a joint checking account, mentally it divides into his, which is used to support the family and hers, which is used to entertain them.

This attitude toward money is buried deep in the traditional terms of marriage in which the woman does not have to work for pay because she has the full responsibilities of being the wife, mother, and homemaker. Any work she does for pay is done out of choice and pursued only so long as it does not in any way hinder her abilities to fulfill her responsibilities at home. It is within this kind of value structure that the notion of "pin money" arises, as well as the notion of women's work as an interest, while man's work is a need.

While their paying work may not be taken as seriously as their husbands', their nonpaid work in the family is. Traditionally the roles of wife and mother are so powerful that a woman does not need a paycheck to exert power and influence in the marriage. Her ability to exercise influence—particularly over the private matters of the family—derives from her domestic roles.

One of the marks of influence for a woman who works for pay at home is her ability to claim work space. What is interesting in Jennifer's case is that historically sewing has been the only work a woman could do that allowed her to claim private space in the home. Except for sewing rooms, the American home has never been designed to give women separate rooms of their own. Men have had studios, libraries, dens, workrooms, and even garages. Children have had bedrooms, which particularly in the middle class are typically not shared, playrooms, and tree houses. But most women have never had a room they could completely call their own. They share their bedrooms with their husbands and they rule over the remainder of the house.

As a result most women who work for pay at home have to carve out a space for themselves that was initially devoted to some other purpose. Typically they take leftover space: a spare bedroom, a corner of the basement; or they share space with other activities in the living or dining room, the master bedroom, the family room, or the recreation room. Jennifer is one of the rare women who displaced family activities in order to provide herself with a room for her work.

She had the conviction that if she was going to work on delicate and valuable fabrics she would need a separate place to keep them. Their three-bedroom ranch house provided no extra room. If she was going to have a separate space with a door, she would have to use one of the bedrooms, which meant putting all three children in one bedroom.

She took the smallest of the three bedrooms and converted it into her sewing room. Facing the front yard, it's filled with morning sun, filtered through the plants that hang in front of the window. A large table holding her sewing machine, telephone, and daily log of work hours sits at right angles to the window. Next to the table stands a tall wardrobe in which she hangs her customers' jobs, and across the room is a hope chest she had covered with cushions to serve as a couch on which the children can sit. A large, comfortable recliner is in the corner.

"I have made this room just like I like it. It is sacred territory. I revere this room to the point where I have two locks on the door. If we go out at night, we make it very clear to the baby-sitter that the kids are not allowed in this room. I have it as a real sanctuary." Every evening after she puts her children to bed, she goes in there to study and prepare her next morning's seminary class. She is up at 4:30 to teach her 6:30 session.

She tries to keep to a schedule, sewing in the mornings from 10:00 to 12:00, in the afternoons from 1:00 to 3:00, and some evenings from 8:00 to 10:00, but she changes her times if the children need something. The children are welcome in her room while she works because normally she can talk to them while she sews, so they never feel entirely left out. It also allows her to work while they are awake, rather than having to work when they are asleep or out of the house. Since there are three of them, they keep themselves occupied playing—and fighting—with each other. She keeps the door open to monitor them and can quickly tell if they need her attention.

Although Jennifer has the workplace she loves and the situation she wants, she operates under no illusions regarding her balancing act. "People think it is a piece of cake working at home, but actually it just creates a different set of problems than what I would have if I worked outside the home." If she worked outside, she would have to find quality child care, but she wouldn't have to take on double duty. "I wouldn't have to worry about taking care of my kids while I worked. Someone else would be doing that." If she worked outside the home, her children would be at a sitter's all day. "The house would be empty and locked up and I'd come home to a clean house. Right now I walk out of my room and the house looks like a disaster struck."

Probably one of the biggest differences is that other people would take her work more seriously. "Most people can't get it through their thick heads that I work since I work at home. Like at my daughter's kindergarten. They asked whether I wanted her in the morning or afternoon session and I said morning. They asked me if I worked and I said yes. Then they asked where and I said at home. They acted like I didn't really work." As a result Jennifer has become an outspoken advocate of women who work in their homes. "I really push the point. I say 'I work.' I don't care where I work, I work."

Working at home has required Jennifer to set limits on what she can accomplish. "You just have to have a basic sense of priority. I can just look at what I have to do that day and set my priorities— I can do this and I can't do that. I can only spend so much time on this and I need to leave that open. If clients call and ask for more, I just say no."

Jennifer has the option to say no because her family is not depending on her income. Although she is very professional and will not disappoint a client to whom she has made a commitment, she has the luxury of turning down clients. Also, because she is happy being at home she feels satisfied in asserting her limits.

The life-style and choices made by Jennifer and Daryl embody the traditional marriage: he is the breadwinner; she is the breadmaker. Just as he is not expected to cook and clean except perhaps to help her out, she is not expected to work for pay, except perhaps for a creative outlet or pin money. Her job is to raise the children, run the house, and tend to the family. When a traditional woman like Jennifer works for pay out of choice, she has the option of quitting any time she feels the work impedes her efforts to be wife, mother, and homemaker.

Years before, Jennifer formed a contract with herself as to what her priorities were and how she should live her life. This was not a written, formal contract that a lawyer drew up and she signed. Rather it was a set of unspoken expectations she had for the kind of woman and wife and mother she should be. Jennifer was brought up believing that she could do and be anything she wanted, but what was more revered than anything else was to be a mother. As she got older her expectations got woven into the patterns of her marriage and her work—often operating outside of conscious awareness, revealing themselves only in side comments such as: "Of course this is what a good mother is. I just couldn't be any other way. I never thought to question it. This is what I was brought up to do." The terms of Jennifer's sense of herself as a woman and wife were tied to her place in the home.

Many women share Jennifer's traditional expectation to marry, bear children, and stay home to raise them. This is the life they wanted and bargained for. Yet, unlike Jennifer, they find midway through their marriages that the terms of their traditional contracts have changed—they must take jobs to help support their families. The Women's Bureau of the U.S. Department of Labor estimates that two out of three working women work out of economic necessity.

Some take jobs outside the home; other women instinctively turn to home-based work as a way to give as little ground as possible as their ideals begin to slip away. Home-based work represents a chance to work but still be home, which is where they want to be. But *having* to work creates a very different situation from wanting to work.

Susan Carlton

Susan is a tall, slender, attractive woman in her early thirties, who lives in a three-bedroom split-level house in a middle-class suburb of St. Louis. She works twenty-five hours a week as a home-based designer doing book layouts for her cousin's printing company. She receives the raw text and turns out a final mechanical layout for the printer. It is precise and skilled work that requires concentration and attention to detail. The path that led Susan to this job began in high school.

When she was a sophomore she started to work as a sales clerk at JC Penney. After graduation she stayed on—not because she particularly liked the work but because nothing else had grabbed her interest. When she was twenty-two she married Michael, was pregnant the next year, and quit her job. "Deciding to quit never fazed me, I guess. I really didn't think too much one way or another about whether I would ever work again."

Like Jennifer, Susan had always assumed that her husband would support the family. She had worked after school just to bide her time, and once married assumed that if she ever worked again, it would be for the same reason. Circumstances proved her wrong. When she was twenty-seven with a four-year-old son and a one-year-old daughter, her husband was unexpectedly laid off. Their large house had a considerable mortgage and, although they had some savings, Susan needed to get a job quickly. Fortunately her cousin needed a technical assistant at that point, and he was willing to train her in the work and let her do it at home.

Susan took the job intending it to be a tide-me-over until her husband could get back on his feet, but discovered that she would have to keep on working when Michael got a new job. His new $27,000-a-year salary was lower than he'd earned before and barely covered their mortgage payment and living expenses. What started out as a temporary arrangement for Susan became permanent, although she continued to have full responsibility for the children and house.

Susan's situation is particularly difficult because she exercises virtually no control over the pace of her work. She never knows when she'll get a project, but when she does, she has less than twenty-four hours to turn it around. She'll get the work in mid-afternoon and have to send it back by the next morning. The combination of housework, child care, lack of control over her work, and lack of sleep have left her with mixed feelings. "My work gives me some self-satisfaction and pride. Before I started working, I didn't think I was doing anything particularly worthwhile in my life. So the work feels good. But on this particular day and this particular week, I'd like to just chuck the whole thing."

It's been difficult for her to admit that working at home is not ideal. Based on what she had heard and read she has the sense that she has a good deal. "Many women dream of having the freedom to be at home, to be able to do things with their kids, and yet be able to earn money." She feels guilty about criticizing it, but the fact is she's having a very difficult time. "I don't want to sound bitter, but the more I thought about what it meant to work at home, the more I realized everything was negative."

A surprising number of women indicate that they feel like failures because they've had such difficulties in managing a job at home. Some of the problems they face are unique to home-based work, but others are shared by all working women, no matter where they work.

One of the toughest problems for Susan has been child care—not a problem one would immediately think of in considering home-based work. Yet in our national survey we found that half of the professional and clerical women with preschool children relied on some form of child care in order to get their work done. Susan's problem is that she doesn't feel justified in paying for help. Although her work enables them to pay the mortgage, she feels that since she is home during the day she shouldn't spend her money for child care. She's also not sure *she* can really afford it. Like many women, traditional and otherwise, she assumes that any child care costs incurred because she is working should be paid only out of her earnings. Although she makes $12 an hour, she doesn't think she earns enough to cover the cost of the Montessori school she'd like her son and daughter to go to. So she cares for the kids herself.

Unlike Jennifer, Susan cannot work while her children are awake and playing around her. Her work requires a concentration and precision that is difficult to sustain when children talk and interrupt. She ends up doing most of her work after the kids go to sleep, which leads to a very long day. "I get up with my husband about 7 A.M, go downstairs about 7:30, get in two hours of work in the morning before my daughter gets up while my son plays in my office with me. He is pretty good. I start work again after they are in bed, and work from about 8:30 or 9:00 P.M. and go until 1 or 2 A.M. Then my husband still expects me to get up at seven and carry on."

She'd like to work during the early evening but has found she can't since her children are more attached to her than they are to her husband. "I try to go downstairs to my office to work while they are up, but I get a million interruptions. It is always, 'Mommy this' and 'Mommy that.' If I try to close and lock my door, they just scream. The fact that I am here means that I am always interrupted."

After trial and error Susan finds that the best time to work is night. "I can get five or six hours of straight time in. So I have no choice. I need five hours to sit and concentrate and get the job done."

This schedule exhausts her and angers her husband because he can't understand why she can't get her work done during the day so she can spend the evening with him. He doesn't seem to take seriously the fact that she has her hands full with the children and house during the day. In fact, Michael feels that she has other reasons for working late at night.

> He's told me that he thinks that I use my work as an excuse to avoid being with him. I said that that wasn't true, but who knows? Maybe I don't spend as much time with him as he thinks I should. That was one of the things he said last night, which made me realize that I never thought about it. He told me that there are some nights when he wants me to go to bed with him, and he thinks that I use work as an excuse not to go to bed together. I never realized that, but maybe subconsciously I have done that in the past. There was never a night where I would pretend that I was working. There might be something that would take me two hours to do that I could do the next morning, but I will do it at night. Maybe he is right.

His overall attitude perplexes her. "He may not like the time I spend working, but he sure likes the money I bring in. I don't understand his reasoning." In a way, his reasoning seems pretty clear—he wants a traditional wife who's there to greet him in the evening *and* he wants a financially contributing partner. In his dual expectations of her he makes the common male assumption that it doesn't really take much effort to run a household and raise children. He doesn't appreciate how hard it is for Susan to do paid work without a front door to separate her from the competing demands of parenting and housework. He thinks that since she's "just staying home" she should be able to do it all.

Without that front door to close, a woman working at home doesn't have the easy ability to concentrate exclusively on her job and ignore the daily household debris of dishes, dust, dirt, and endless tasks calling for attention. Without the symbolism of walking out the front door to "go to work," she finds that people are tempted to think she is "staying home," rather than "working." Both family and friends are not as apt to take her and her work as seriously as they would if she worked outside.

Susan has grown increasingly resentful of her husband's critical attitude and feels he has a much easier life because he works a five-day work week. "He can leave his job at the end of the day and say good-bye until the next morning. He knows he never has to work on weekends. There are a lot of weekends that I have to spend at home working, instead of going out and doing something. I never know exactly when I am going to get a job to do."

Susan has forfeited her position of "not working," and gotten in way over her head. She feels stressed, overextended, and confused. The whole middle ground—the question of who is responsible for housework and child care—has never been renegotiated or discussed in any definitive fashion. In fact, her husband has started to use his assistance in the evening as a bargaining chip to get her to stop work in time to go to bed with him. Many of their arguments are the result of a failure in this barter system. "If I've asked my husband to watch the kids, he gets ticked off if I *don't* finish by eleven." She thinks his help is no more than a token gesture, anyway. "Asking him to watch the kids is a joke. I get paid by the hour, so every time I get interrupted I have to write it down on my log. Some nights there are twenty entries in a matter of two hours. There are times when I feel bitter."

It is hard for Susan to do anything to change the arrangement because she does feel it is her responsibility to care, cook, and clean. She has so internalized these responsibilities that she herself is not clear about the need to renegotiate the terms of responsibility for housework and child care. "I don't have the time to do everything I have to do. There are times when my husband comes home from work and I haven't even been able to start dinner. If I am not here to do it, then who is going to?"

She continues to feel that all of the housework and child care is her responsibility: "I am not working full-time, so I guess that the housework is part of my job." Yet she would like Michael to offer to help her out with her responsibilities: "If he would just offer, just once, to push the vacuum around, to run to the store, to clean a toilet, it would make all the difference in the world. I don't want to have to be a nagging witch, but if he would just take the time to offer once in a while, that would be the most wonderful thing in the world."

Although she wants things to change, it is more of a wish than a demand.

I wish there was some way that society had brought us all up so that men could take turns with women. A lot of women carry on in the same job a man has, but I don't think men really conceive of what women do all day at home. Whether it is cleaning the toilet, scouring the sink, doing laundry every single day, washing the same dishes every single day—all those sorts of things. I think everybody should go through that.

Susan is frustrated and angry yet neither she nor her husband has focused on the fact that their traditional roles have changed because she is working for pay. She has forfeited the privileges of a full-time homemaker—the privilege of not having a paid job—but has retained all of the full-time homemaker's responsibilities as wife, mother, and housekeeper. Michael, on the other hand, has willingly accepted her contributions to the household income— her taking on some of his responsibilities as sole breadwinner—but has failed to relinquish any of his privileges, such as not having to be responsible for housework or child care. All the tensions in the family seem to be focused on *her* failure to be the nurturing wife, the full-time mother, and the spotless housekeeper. No one has addressed the fact that he has failed to uphold his traditional role as sole provider.

Anne Michado

Anne Michado is as angry as Susan, but her anger is not focused on her husband. In her mind our society is to blame.

A first-generation American, Anne was raised in a deeply religious Italian community in the Bronx where the emphasis was on family and hard work. Although always industrious, Anne did not have career aspirations when she graduated from high school. She took a clerk-typist job with a New York City bank with every intention of quitting as soon as she got married. Unlike Susan, she began to enjoy her work and so she kept working after her wedding. Eventually she reached the highest rung of the secretarial ladder, looked higher, and saw that she couldn't go any further. After twelve years with the bank, she painfully realized that she never would be promoted out of the ranks of secretary. "Here I was running this branch. I could do *all* the jobs, but I was constantly being passed over for promotions." Bank management finally made it explicit that unless she went back to school and got her college degree, she would stay right where she was.

By this time Anne was thirty. She had been married for five years and had worked at the bank long enough to be fully vested in the pension plan. She decided to forgo college—and a career—and focus instead on her family. "Sure I was a little bitter, but I had always wanted to have children, so I decided that this was the time to get pregnant."

Anne and her husband assumed that once she gave birth, she would raise their child and not work for pay. But economic circumstances intervened. Her husband was temporarily laid off from his job as a building maintenance supervisor; she developed costly medical complications during her pregnancy, and having an infant daughter was proving more expensive than they had expected: "Money-wise, things got pretty rough." Shortly after her daughter's birth Anne decided she had to find a part-time job.

She was less troubled by the prospect of working than Susan because she had always enjoyed having a job. But the reality of the part-time job market turned her sour on the idea of working outside the home.

Since they had no car, Anne took the best job she could find on their bus route: as a cashier earning minimum wage at a local fast-food store. In order to save baby-sitting expenses, she worked nights. As a result she almost never saw her husband. He'd walk in at five, just as she walked out to work. After several months, Anne decided to find a job she could do at home, scheduled around her nine-month-old's sleeping schedule. She happened on her job by reading want ads in the local paper.

"Finally, I saw an ad for a home typist. They offered pick-up and delivery and it seemed perfect. I answered the ad, went down and took a typing test from a dictaphone, passed, and was hired. They explained that I would be paid fifty cents a page and two cents a line for anything over two pages. It ends up that I average about $5 an hour," which is over a dollar more than she earned as a cashier. Out of these earnings she paid $65 a month for rental for the specific kind of typewriter required.

She thought she was an employee. Although the company told her they weren't going to take out taxes, Anne didn't realize that meant she was being hired as a self-employed "independent contractor." She only realized her status a year later at tax time, when her husband took their forms to H & R Block. Then she began to tally the costs and benefits of this arrangement over that of being a company employee.

Anne is paid for each page she types and not by a salary. She gets paid only for the amount of work she does, not for any lag times between work, nor does she get any paid vacations or sick leave. She receives no health insurance or pension coverage, and she pays more for her Federal social security account than she would as an employee. As a self-employed contractor, she pays 12.3 percent of her earnings for social security, whereas if she was an employee, she would pay 7.15 percent and her employer would contribute the difference. Her employer also makes no contributions to any other government protection for her. If she ever hurt herself doing her work, she wouldn't be eligible to collect workman's compensation, or if her company stopped giving her work, she couldn't collect any unemployment insurance. Despite the fact that she is not paid or protected like an employee would be, Anne works under very employee-like conditions. A courier drops off and picks up work every day. She is expected to complete it within twenty-four hours, and she has to follow the guidelines laid out by her employer. The question is obvious: Why is she putting up with conditions that expect her to perform as an employee, but that don't recompense her as such? The answer is simple. She has no other option. Despite all the public talk about companies hiring home workers, according to a recent study fewer than three hundred companies hire people to work at home. It is not easy to find a job at home and Anne considers herself lucky to have found anything.

If Anne wants to work at home she has few job options in the marketplace other than starting a business, which would require more time, energy, and capital than she has. The beginning entrepreneur can spend twelve to fifteen hours a day starting a business, and Anne does not have the resources or the inclination to do that. Her situation is not unique. Insurance companies, typing services, transcription services, and manufacturers hire mothers as independent contractors to work in their homes. In fact, some companies change the status of their workers from employees to contractors when the worker moves from the office to the home.

Controversy exists over whether these women are really independent contractors or whether companies call them that simply to avoid paying the benefits and salaries they'd pay them as office employees, thereby saving thirty to fifty percent on each worker hired as a contractor. A case pending in the California courts challenges the corporate practice of contracting out work to home-based workers.

In 1982, California Western States Life Insurance Company offered some of its insurance-claims processors the opportunity to do their work at home instead of in the office. They would become contractors, paid by a piece rate and given no benefits. The processors, most of them women with family responsibilities, saw it as an attractive option—at first. They could have more flexibility and save the money and time previously spent commuting. Most of them joined the program in 1983.

On December 1, 1985, eight of the women quit their jobs and filed a suit against the company, claiming that the independent contracting arrangement was simply a subterfuge to avoid paying them benefits. They also claimed that the company kept increasing their quotas, sometimes forcing them to work 15 hours a day, eliminating any flexibility. Together, they are seeking $250,000 in back benefits and at least $1 million in punitive damages. The women are claiming fraud on the part of the company. California Western's position is that the plaintiffs signed the contracts, knew what they were getting, and always had the right to quit.

This case illustrates some of the pitfalls of contracting out work. The legal status of independent contractors is ambiguous, and has been made more so by recent revisions to the tax code. Under common law, the question of whether a worker is an employee or an independent contractor generally revolves around the following questions:

—How much control does the worker have over the execution of the work?

—What is the worker's opportunity for profit or loss?

—Has the worker made a large investment in the enterprise? Does he or she have a place of business and offer services to the public?

—What is the worker's level of skill?

—How permanent is the relationship?

Generally, an independent contractor exercises control over the execution and timing of the work, has the opportunity to gain or lose, has made an investment in equipment or capital, has a skill that allows him or her to compete in the marketplace, and is not in an enduring relationship with the employer.

The corollary holds true. If the worker has little control over work hours, priority, or pacing of the work, has no opportunity to gain or lose, uses materials, tools, or equipment from the employer, and has an ongoing relationship with the company, then he or she is entitled to the rights and protection accorded by law to company employees.

Based on these legal criteria the women in California argue they should have been employees, not contractors. They had the financial resources to challenge the practice, but most other contractors are in Anne's financial position, and unable to consider legal action that would jeopardize their jobs.

Anne knows that she has made certain trade-offs by working as a home-based contractor but sees it as the best of her alternatives. "I get low pay, boring work, no opportunities for advancement, and no benefits, but I get to stay home with my daughter." And working at home seems easier than working either part-time or full-time outside of it. "I don't know if I could handle a full-time job outside. I'd have to leave the house at seven. Then I'd come home at six or seven and then I'd have to cook and take care of the family. I don't think I could do that. That is just more pressure on top of pressure."

We have found that three out of four home-based working women assume overall responsibility for housework. The only task their husbands are likely to take on is emptying the garbage. It is not surprising, then, that many women make the decision to work at home. A full-time job outside the home would be too demanding and a part-time job would probably not pay enough to make it worthwhile. Given these options Anne sees that, all things considered, working at home is suited to her needs at this time in her life.

Yet, the arrangement has it own pressures. In order to get the work finished, she ends up with a grueling schedule. When she first started as a home-based typist Anne worked for an hour in the afternoon while her infant napped, then fixed dinner, cleaned up, bathed her, put her to bed and sat down to work again at 7:00 in the evening. Spurred by her deadlines, she'd work until 2:00 or 3:00 in the morning, then get back up at 6:00 to see her husband off and care for her daughter. After six months of getting three or four hours of sleep a night, she quit.

Anne waited until her daughter was three years old and could go to a play school three mornings a week before she started typing again. She now types during the morning hours, and again in the evenings from 7:00 until 12:00 or 1:00 in the morning. Having additional daytime hours did not eliminate her night work, but shortened it. Unlike Susan Carlton, she can work in the evening because her husband usually watches their child. The two of them go upstairs to the family room and watch television or read. She finds it very hard some evenings to stay at her kitchen desk typing when she knows that they're curled up on the couch watching TV.

Despite the mixed blessing of her arrangement, overall she likes having her typing job—it gives her something to do besides housework. "There's only so much cooking and cleaning I can do." Yet she is angry at what she feels are our society's unrealistic demands on women. "Just being a housewife is not supposed to be enough, you know? We're expected to take care of the family, run the house, and hold a job."

Anne is angry about the way the advertising media portrays housewives as dumb and working women as better. She particularly hated the TV ad several years ago that had a tall, leggy brunette crooning, "I can bring home the bacon, fry it up in a pan, and never let him forget that he's a man."

"I go 'Goddamn it, will you listen to this? They make it sound like you love doing all that, and you *don't.*' It really bugs me; it just upsets me. I wish I could win the lottery and then we'd be comfortable, but I can't."

The reality is that Anne no longer has the choice whether or not to work. She has been able to choose to work at home, but feels that the difficulty of trying to separate work and family makes it even harder than working outside.

> You're juggling so many things, and it's constantly there. When you're in an office, the only thing you really do is work. You might think of the house, and say, Oh God, I've got to cook something for dinner, or Did I defrost the roast? But when you get up to go get a soda from the soda machine, that's all you're doing. At home I get up to get a soda, and the refrigerator says, "Better clean me." Or I go to the bathroom and I think, I better clean that. It's always there, hitting me in the face.

Since she is "at home" Anne has in fact assumed much more of the responsibility for housework than she did when both she and her husband worked outside. "The reason is simple. My husband goes to work, and I do not. I am home twenty-four hours a day and things kind of slip back to the age when the mother was always at home with the children. Slowly it turns back to that. I think even women begin to think like that. 'It is more of a woman's job to take care of the house and family.' We just slip back into it."

Anne makes herself feel better about the toll working at home has taken on her by arguing that women are more adaptable than men:

> My husband could never do what I do. I don't think he could keep up the pace I do, getting only four or five hours of sleep every night for a year and a half. He needs more sleep than that; he konks out at ten or eleven and sleeps until six. We women can handle more. I think we are built differently. Maybe it is just because of the sense of family, but it makes us push harder. I think women adapt better than men. I just think women are more resilient.

The notions of adaptability, strength, and resiliency all carry very positive meanings. Yet they obscure the reality that women like Anne are exhausted and are getting limited help from their spouses. Although they may help out with the children as Anne's husband willingly does, they don't pitch in with the cooking, cleaning, shopping, or worrying about getting it all done. Rather than confronting or criticizing their partners for being inflexible or unhelpful, the women make a virtue out of the fact that they are so adaptable. Adaptability becomes a valued feminine quality. But in another way it becomes a survival technique, because making the family and marriage work is their primary goal. If their husbands are unwilling to confront or deal with the problems, the women have two options: force the issue with their husbands, at the risk of making everyone unhappy and possibly jeopardizing their marriages; or take on more of the responsibilities themselves and turn their ability to do so into a virtue.

At some point, all the traditional women interviewed for this book tried the first option, but they all eventually tired of the struggle. They got worn down by having to fight on top of everything else—working, houseworking, and taking care of the children. Most end up with the second option, without realizing in the long run how destructive it is for them. Marnie Baker has begun to realize this.

Marnie Baker

At 38, Marnie Baker lives in the Silicon Valley with her husband and children, a daughter and a son. Her entire work life has been spent in the insurance industry, processing insurance claims.

At 18, she started working as a claims clerk. Over the next several years, she started and stopped college several times, always returning to the claims rating. "I really didn't know what I wanted to do. Sometimes I think at nineteen you don't know what you want to do. You know you are supposed to be in college because you took college prep all through high school, but you find yourself sitting in a college class and listening to a boring professor." Without a clear purpose, Marnie found little incentive to finish college, so quit and worked as a claims rater.

She married Cal at 21 and found herself increasingly bored with her job. "I practically fell asleep at my desk. Then I got pregnant." In retrospect Marnie speculates: "Sometimes I wonder if you get pregnant to get out of jobs you don't like." In the course of this research, many traditional women spoke of how they used pregnancy to escape a dead-end job. Others spoke of getting pregnant at times when they were unsure or unclear as to what they wanted to do with their own lives.

Getting pregnant gave them a good reason to leave a job, and also gave them a definite and important purpose. It also allowed them to put off having to face decisions regarding their individual lives. But it is a circular situation in which they have found themselves. Since Marnie always expected to quit once she got pregnant, she never had the incentive to devote herself to a career that might have resulted in a more interesting job. Had she had a job that challenged her more she might not have turned to pregnancy as an escape hatch.

She quit the company and went home in her sixth month of pregnancy, saying, "Why stay until nine months? I didn't have anything to prove that I could make it to the end." She gave birth to her first child in 1974 and her second in 1977. During their early years she was quite content to stay home.

Like many women, when Marnie wanted some pin money, she would baby-sit for neighbor women who worked. At first she thought it would be ideal: she wouldn't have to invest any money to start the work; she could pick it up and put it down when she wanted; and she could do it while she was taking care of her own children thereby preserving the life-style she wanted. It seemed to be a relatively easy thing to take on. Marnie baby-sat off and on for ten years but grew to despise the toll it took on her and her family.

"The kids were all over the house. They nearly destroyed the walls. They were all on different eating, sleeping, and school bus schedules. I hated it and my husband hated it and I got to the point where I didn't even enjoy my own kids. I was 'kidded' out." Rather than enhancing her life-style as a wife and mother, she felt that baby-sitting was destroying her. She finally decided she would rather do without extra spending money than put herself through it anymore. She quit baby-sitting and enjoyed being a full-time home-maker until the early 1980s, when the volatility of the Silicon Valley economy touched her family.

The computer company her husband worked for went bankrupt and he was out of a job with no prospects in sight. Marnie was forced into action, and decided to find a full-time job outside the home so that the family would have a salary and health benefits. Drawing on her earlier experience as an insurance claims rater, she took the first rating job she was offered, even though it meant a sixty-minute commute in solid traffic each way.

She quickly discovered that taking a job outside the house did not eliminate any of her family duties. Although both she and her husband came home from full-time jobs, she was the one who cooked dinner, cleaned up, helped her sons with their homework and got them off to bed. Furthermore, she came to believe that she wasn't really earning enough to make it either financially or emo-tionally worthwhile for her to work full-time. After her expenses for commuting, child care, and lunches were paid, she cleared less than $50 a week. "It just wasn't worth it," she said. "I don't know why I put myself through such torture."

Part of the reason it was torture was that while she was adding on job responsibilities, she was not relinquishing any of the high standards she had set for herself when she was home full-time. She had a strong, almost rigid, idea of what a good mother should be—and once she started working she felt she rarely measured up.

A *good mother* has everything done. She has got it all under control. When I worked outside the home I didn't have it under control at all. The kids didn't get a hot meal, the house was in shambles, and I just felt like everything was out of control. I wanted to do certain things for my kids and I just couldn't. I mean, if you feel comfortable not having a good hot meal for your kids at dinner that is great, but I come from an era where you *had* to have and you *wanted* to have a nice hot dinner for them. Something as minor as that really upset me! I know a girl who works and fixes a peanut butter sandwich for her kids at night. Her kids seem happy. They are not dying of starvation. Everybody is happy, but that would make me very unhappy.

Marnie couldn't keep up with all of the expectations that she had for herself. Although she says, "I wish the idea of the *good mother* would fly out the window," she acknowledges that, "It is very hard to change where you came from and what you're expected to do."

Her husband did little to alleviate her sense of responsibility and failure when she was working, partly because he was home so little during the week. He had taken a part-time computer consulting job that required him to travel several days each week, throwing all the family responsibilities onto her. Her company's policies on work schedules only made things harder. "You know you had to almost grovel to get time off to take your kids to the doctor. It was depressing. Who needs it?" She couldn't let go, her husband didn't help, and her employer was inflexible. As soon as her husband found a steady job, Marnie quit.

She felt that the only way she'd ever be a good mother was if she devoted her full time and energy to it. Although being home meant she could be the good mother she wanted to be, Marnie soon discovered that this might not be good for her own emotional well-being.

I kept falling asleep on the couch at two in the afternoon. I said, You better start to do something, because you are not going to sit around here and fall asleep on the couch. I didn't know what I would do, but I did know I was bored. It's scary, because you start to think that you are not doing anything, that you are dull.

And you look at other women and you think, they're going here and they're going there. And you are not.

Marnie found that she was not only bored but angry at the idea that she might waste her life. "I thought, I've got something to offer out there. I don't think it would be a good idea for me to just sit here." She worried that her husband would be very upset with her and that her kids would wonder about her, too, because they were used to her working.

She was caught in a double bind: when she worked outside of the home, she was tortured by guilt for not living up to her idea of a good mother. But when she quit, went home, and met those expectations, she felt bored, under-utilized, and sensed that her loved ones were not proud of her. In fact, her husband frequently told her that he liked her better when she was working outside the home. "My husband knows that when I work full-time I take very good care of myself. He likes to see me get dressed up and look like a woman. He knows when I turn on my work personality, and he likes that personality."

But as much as Cal might like that personality, he had shown that he was not willing to put in time on the house and the kids so she could have a job. "Those are not things that he wants to do. He doesn't like that part." Marnie had accepted that she was in a sense "responsible for the whole family."

I am the emotional mainstay. Sometimes, it is a drag. I wish I could have my little temper tantrums. I used to have a fantasy of just getting in my car and leaving, and saying "FUCK IT." It is a drag being responsible for everybody. But this is my role in life.

Given her role, Marnie eventually decided to work at home, as it seemed the best way to have a job and still fulfill her responsibilities as wife and mother. She answered an ad in the local newspaper for home-based insurance raters and was hired as an independent contractor under arrangements virtually identical to Anne's.

Yet, in contrast to Anne, Marnie has no pre-school-age children, which made it easier for her to work during the day, from nine to three. Until recently, her home-based job was pursued out of choice. Yet, last year economic circumstances again changed her situation from one of choice to one of necessity.

> When I first started working at home, my husband had a very good job, paying very nicely. My income was to help do the private school bit. My older child was going to be graduating from her private school and would have to go to another one, so we were looking for one. It was going to be almost $350 a month for one child, and $300 for the other. I said to Cal, "It's time to put them back in public school, and start using that money to fix up our house. I mean, I have been sacrificing long enough. It is time to get this house together." And he said "You're right," so that is what we were planning to do. Then he got laid off. I mean, all my plans went out the door. And I thought, oh, my God, what's going to happen now? He was only off for a month or so, thank God. But he had to take a pay cut. At first, he went down from $40,000 to I think $35,000, and that's a big cut. But I thought, oh well, the $5,000 I'm getting from this work will make up the difference. But two months after he had taken that job, they said, "Listen guys, we're gonna have to cut back every-body's salary, because we're hardly making it." So we went down even further. So, now he's down to about $24,000 a year. If I put in my $5,000, we're down from a total last year of $45,000 to less than $30,000 this year. That's a big change in my standard of living.

Marnie's initial reaction was to get more rating work to do at home, and her supervisor, Glenda, helped out as best she could. But Marnie quickly began to realize that "independent contracting" was not going to meet their needs. Contracting is great for the employer, because they don't have to pay for any lag time between projects, but it wreaks havoc on a family that needs a dependable income. Marnie found that she could never rely on a stable check. She might earn $200 every two weeks, then go down to $150 every two weeks. What's more, she saw the situation getting worse rather than better, since many insurance companies are phasing out their home-based raters as they computerize their personal rating systems. For the first time in her life Marnie has had to develop a strategy regarding her work.

I have to have something that's going to be stable. I am going to have to go back to work. I mean I get teary-eyed when I start to think about it, because I really don't want to get out there and work every day, but I know I have got to go.

But she also is getting more explicit about the kind of job arrangements she'll accept.

I told my husband that I am not going to commute an hour and a half away from home. I'm going to take my time and not accept the first job that comes along just because I am scared to death that nothing else will come along. I'd like to make sure that the new company would guarantee that they'll train me in commercial rating—no more of this personal time. I'd be willing to start off in personal rating, but I want to make sure that they can get me into commercial lines. I'd make more money in commercial and I'd have more job security. Personal lines are getting more computerized and there's not too much job security there.

Yet the prospects of a full-time paying job outside the home and a full-time nonpaying job at home do not please her.

I know what I have to look forward to. It's not like I don't know what's going to happen when I go to work. What's going to happen is I'm going to come home at five o'clock tired; there's going to be kids wanting attention; there's going to be a husband who's going to come home tired, too; there's going to be slop. I mean, nothing will be done the way I like things done. Everybody will be trying, but I like things done my way and that's why I will have to learn how to say, Well, I'll settle for what I can get.

Marnie imagines that she'll be able to adjust, but her sense of responsibility is so deeply ingrained that she also realizes that it's going to be difficult for her to relinquish her control over housework and family. She clearly does not relish the prospect. "I am not looking forward to this. It's like you have to change all the rules and everybody in the whole family has to think of new ways of doing things." This means that Marnie has to learn to accept her husband as a full partner in the house.

I will have to learn to be okay with how Cal does things. He doesn't do things when I say to do them. I want them done now, but he will wait to get around to doing it. I am just going to have to learn not to say to him, "Gosh, can't you do it now?" Take this for example. On Saturday mornings, when I get up, I have grocery shopping to do, cleaners to go to, and all that. It takes a big chunk out of my day. The floor needs to be mopped. I have to make a choice which one I'm going to do. He says, "I won't do your grocery shopping, I can't stand grocery shopping." Okay, that leaves mopping the floor. So he says, "Well, I will mop the floor, but I'm not going to do it right away on Saturday. I'll wait until later." Yeah, he'll wait until ten o'clock at night when everybody else is trying to do something else. Now see, I won't go for that. I want it done Saturday morning, while I am out shopping and doing other things. Get all the housework done in the morning. That's the way I grew up. When you grow up that way, that's the way you want everything to go. I mean, on Saturday mornings, we got up, had breakfast, and did our chores. We didn't wait until ten o'clock at night. We didn't sit there and read a book while everybody else was working. You had better get up and start moving. My father would have had a fit. But I don't think it's going to work with Cal too well. It's one way of his saying he's in charge and this is the way he wants to do it.

Marnie and Cal are in the midst of renegotiating entire domains of their relationship. She is setting the terms under which she will take a job in order to help support the family, and he is setting the terms under which he will do housework to help support the family. Each has ventured into the traditional turf of the other and both are determined to hold their ground. Marnie sees what is going on as "a war of wills, and the question is 'Who will win?'" She sees paid help as providing the way out of this battle.

Hiring somebody would probably be the easiest way to go. Just pay someone to clean the house. I would have to bring home some type of salary to be able to afford it, but I think that is the best solution. We're not going to get a divorce over housework. That would be a very stupid thing to get a divorce over.

Her strategy for peace is not exactly a negotiation—it's more of a way to avoid underlying issues regarding power and control in the family. Marnie intends to solve the power struggle by earning enough money to hire a housekeeper. Like the women who feel they have to earn enough to pay for child care themselves, Marnie feels that she has to be financially responsible for housekeeping costs.

Cal is in full agreement about hiring a housekeeper. He can't understand why I haven't ever had one before. He fully understands why a woman would not want to do housework all day. He doesn't understand why I feel I must do things my way. I think that it is the martyr in me, you know, the belief that I must suffer. But why pay somebody to do something that you could do yourself? When I look at it, I think he is right.

In the midst of thinking through new ways to run their home, Marnie has had new ideas about the marketplace and how it is set up. "You know, there's a real class system out there. If you do not have a college degree you don't go anywhere." She needs another year and a half of courses to finish her bachelor's degree, yet she feels that her family could not get along without her income for that long, so she dreams about taking evening courses, but realizes that with both job and family responsibilities she really wouldn't have the energy to go to school as well.

Like many traditional women, as a young woman Marnie never planned to work after she had her children. As a result, she made few plans for developing highly paid skills. But the economy changed and two incomes became a necessity, not a luxury. Women like Marnie now find themselves with few options for advancement—without college degrees or training it will be hard for them to develop fulfilling ways to work or to have many options about the nature of their work. Fortunately, Marnie has begun to think about her future in terms of what she wants and how she can get it. Her dream is at some point to go back and get her college degree.

All of the women in this chapter were determined to stay home and raise their children. At the time they married, none thought they would ever *have* to work for pay again. Although Jennifer's family circumstances have allowed her to be the traditional homemaker and do her sewing for extra spending money, the other three— Susan, Anne, and Marnie—are in different economic situations. Despite the differences among them, they share a number of similarities.

Their husbands have not been able to earn enough so the women can be the non-earning homemakers they had expected to be. The women started to work at home as a way of helping out for what they thought would be a short-term arrangement. They had no sense of planning or organization for the job. They fell into the work bit by bit out of necessity, without any model of how they should set it up. As a result, none of the three had any clear boundaries around their jobs—in terms of space, time, or their identities. Without boundaries, they didn't have a platform from which to renegotiate their agreements with their husbands regarding housework and child care.

The extent to which they lack boundaries, as well as a platform for negotiating, can be contrasted to the situation of a New York psychoanalyst who had both the traditional breadwinning role and the professional training to justify his demands for working at home.

Alex Lucas was born in 1924 and raised to believe that he should earn enough money to support his family. In the late forties, he married a woman who also believed in the traditional division of roles. Their agreement was simple, straightforward, and entirely in line with the norms of that time—he would be the breadwinner and his wife would be the non-earning homemaker.

During the early years of their marriage he trained as a classic psychoanalyst. When he started to practice, they did not have enough money for him to rent office space so they decided he would use part of their Manhattan apartment for his office.

Starting with Sigmund Freud, psychoanalysts often have set up their offices in their homes, and the classic analytic tradition actually specifies very strict rules regarding how offices should be designed. For example, one patient should never see another, which means that the entrance and exit must be separate.

To provide this, Alex cordoned off the front end of their apartment. The front door led to his waiting room, which opened onto the treatment room, from which another door exited back out into the elevator area. This design limited the movements of his wife and infant daughter. They could only use the front door when it did not conflict with the arrivals and departures of patients. All other times, they had to use the back door and the service elevator.

When he was earning enough to afford a separate office space, he moved his practice across town. The boundaries between his work and his family were just as strictly guarded there as they had been when his offices were in his apartment. One morning he was already across town and in session with his 7:00 A.M. appointment when his five-year-old daughter fell out of bed and broke her collarbone. Rather than interrupt her husband, his wife went to a next-door neighbor for help. Although both she and her husband now marvel that she would have relied on a neighbor before she'd interrupt her husband, they also realized that in those days his work boundaries were not to be trespassed no matter what the emergency. His work was their means of survival and his training was very strict regarding the boundaries around his work.

Few traditional women who work at home are as empowered as breadwinners or professionals to establish boundaries with that kind of authority. The women in this chapter have simply added on paid work to their traditional responsibilities at home, rather than insisting that those responsibilities be renegotiated. They don't feel justified in asserting the need to do so and continue to think of themselves as "traditional women" though they clearly are not.

When a woman works for pay at home under conditions of necessity she no longer is the traditional woman. No tradition exists that expects a woman to do all the housework, all the child care, *and* take on a job and earn enough to pay for any help she needs with cleaning or caretaking. When a woman accepts those terms she becomes both the homemaker and breadwinner, while her husband remains only the breadwinner. The bargain is not equitable.

The only way women will rectify this unfair distribution of responsibilities is when they admit it's a problem, talk to their husbands, and begin to renegotiate the terms of their marriage contracts. If they're going to contribute to the financial support of their families, the husbands must contribute to the cooking and cleaning. Women may marry for better or for worse, but not for all the work.

3

Career Women Who Need to Raise Their Children

In contrast to the homemakers of the first chapter, some career women never intended to quit their jobs and "stay home." They had spent years advancing in their careers, seeing each educational and job decision as a step in a sequence leading to greater and greater success. Their energies, their hearts, and their identities were heavily invested in their work, though they never assumed that professional success should be the price of family life. For the most part they married men who shared their belief that work and family do not preclude one other. It came as quite a surprise to many of these couples that their plans did not mesh with the realities of having a baby.

Although heralded as the first generation with choice—to work or not to work, to take time off to raise children or not—these women will tell you that they did not feel like they really had free choice. Pulled between the desire to work and the desire to be home to raise their children, they found no easy solution in the world of conventional work. For many working at home appeared to offer an ideal way to satisfy the need to be "a good mother" and the need to be a career woman.

Lisa Jacobi

Back when she was 22, Lisa Jacobi would have been shocked to hear that one day she would quit her job to stay home and raise her daughters. She had just graduated from college and had been hired as a management trainee with the East Coast offices of AT&T and had every intention of working her way up the corporate ladder. Over the next eight years, she did exactly that, eventually being promoted to the position of regional manager.

> I had to meet regularly with managers and employees in our stores. It required me to be on the road a lot. I loved my job. I loved working with people. I always felt like I was on stage.

During that time, she met and married Stewart, an economist who worked for the federal government. From the onset they had an explicit understanding that in their marriage they were full partners—both in the workplace and in the home. Neither's career would be subordinated to the other's. Since their incomes were virtually identical it was easy to avoid the trap of assuming that the person with the higher income should exercise more power in the family's decision making. Although Lisa continued to assume overall responsibility for the house, Stewart took on many of the tasks so that the burdens were more evenly divided than in most traditional marriages. Given the importance of both their careers and the parity of their relationship it was assumed that both would continue to work after they had children. "I always thought it wouldn't be a big deal, that somehow I'd juggle everything," said Lisa.

When she was 32, Lisa gave birth to their daughter, Ellen. To Lisa's surprise and bewilderment, becoming a parent caused her to re-evaluate their situation. While on maternity leave she began to take a hard look at her job and its travel demands. Despite her hopes of continuing to work she had to accept the fact that "a baby doesn't adhere to any type of schedule." Her company offered no child care assistance, so she spent the first months of her maternity leave scouting for child care. She was horrified at what she saw, finding some unfit "even for a dog." A more fundamental re-evaluation was the result of an intense re-experiencing of her own childhood. "My mom was always there when we got home. We were always able to burst in the door and tell her what we did. I remember how annoyed I was the few times she wasn't at home. How dare she not be home? I wanted my mother to be there."

She began to translate these memories into guides for her own life as a mother and became convinced that staying home was the only way that she could provide the moral guidance she wanted to give her children. "If you have a set of values that are real important you want to be able to transfer them to your children. If you are away from home forty to fifty hours a week, then someone else is influencing your children a lot more than you are."

She and Stewart came to the conclusion that one of them had to stay home. Unlike the majority of husbands who would not contemplate altering their careers for their children, Stewart was willing to be the prime nurturer and would have been able to, since he had accrued extensive leave time. But to add to Lisa's confusion, she found that she couldn't accept that possibility or its implications.

> I know that this feeling of mine isn't innate, that it comes from all the conditioning I had as a kid. *Mothers* were always the ones who stayed home and took care of the kids. When Stewart offered to do that, I could not accept the idea that he'd be the mom and I'd be the breadwinner. I just couldn't reconcile that switch within myself.

But she wasn't sure she could stay home either. Therefore, she approached her employer to see if they'd let her work at home. But the novelty of the situation—and the difficulties of creating a job that she could do at home and figuring out how to supervise her— prompted them to say no. It became clear that if she wanted to stay home, she would have to quit altogether. The prospect did not please her. In fact, it terrified her. Her career meant so much to her—it had provided her with a sense of power and status; it had given her the income that she felt was an important factor in the sense of equality she felt with her husband. The regularity of a paycheck provided a sustained sense of self-esteem and independence.

I had had a paycheck since I was sixteen. Now, all of a sudden, I had to decide for the first time in my life not to have a job and to depend on someone else for support. I know that there's no logic to it. I know that when you're at home you work, but I think that having that paycheck in my name was real important. I just knew that I needed to feel like I was contributing to the support of our household. I've always felt like that—even as a kid. I just can't get the words out to ask for money.

It was a difficult and confusing time for her. She was unsure about giving up her job but couldn't see how she could maintain her dual and competing allegiances to her employer and her child.

I didn't think it was fair to go back to the company. I had such loyalty to them. Before I had my children, I was able to commit long hours. After Ellen was born, I couldn't commit the same type of hours. I had to be with her. I knew that I just couldn't give the company one hundred percent like I had before.

Many career women feel that if they go back to work for their company after the birth of their child they can no longer give as much—in hours or emotional commitment—as they did before. In their minds anything less than 100 percent is unacceptable, an attitude apparently shared by most employers.

Although her employer offered Lisa several jobs during her maternity leave none would have fit her schedule as a parent—all of them would have required extensive travel and overtime. Although flattered that the company obviously didn't want to lose her—she loved working for them and wanted to continue—she saw no alternative but to quit since they offered no middle ground short of full-time nine-to-five commitment, which would have made it impossible to give what she needed to give to parenting. Had her employer had the flexibility to offer Lisa job-sharing, part-time work, or, even more radically, a full-time job with hours synchronized to the daily and seasonal clock of child care, school, and summer vacations, they could have retained the skilled services and invaluable enthusiasm of an experienced employee.

Instead, Lisa had to choose between herself and her child. She quit her job. "I went through what I guess a lot of women go through—wondering if you're doing the right thing. Are you being selfish if you work? Are you giving enough time to your kids?" Although she left her job, Lisa knew she could not be a full-time mother—she had to earn money.

Working at home seemed to offer what she needed. She could earn money and yet avoid being typecast completely as a homemaker, a role she had assiduously avoided her entire life.

One of the most striking aspects of Lisa's search for suitable home-based work was her loss of confidence and direction. Although she had over ten years of business experience, she initially saw no way to translate that experience into a home-based business. Instead, she began a frantic search of newspaper ads to find *any* kind of work she could do at home.

> I wasn't proud. I'd do anything. I just needed to prove to myself that I could do something at home and use the skills that I had spent all those years acquiring. I found a secondhand store through the newspaper that wanted someone who could call up people and ask for donations. They hired me and I did it two hours in the morning and two hours at night. On Sunday nights, Stewart would help. I only made a little money, but that was all I needed to know—that I could do something at home.

Unlike the women in Chapter 1, who stayed with the jobs they found through want ads, Lisa used the telephone job to gain enough confidence to figure out her next step. She became convinced she wanted to start a business. Her husband's personal computer seemed the natural starting point for one, and she knew Stewart would show her how to use it.

The computer has been hailed by some as the basis for a greatly expanded home-based work industry in the future. In Lisa's case the computer was essential and made her business possible. But our research indicates that in the vast majority of cases, the computer plays a minimal role in the decision to work at home or in the home-based job. Only one in four clerical workers uses one, as does only one in three professional workers. More frequently the decision to work at home is based on family or business reasons. Once the decision has been made the question becomes: "What kind of work?" The computer offers potential, but so does the typewriter, paper, and pencil. To focus so much attention on the computer is to ignore the real reasons why people are working at home—as Lisa's case illustrates. Her decision had nothing to do with technology and everything to do with her values regarding child-rearing. Although the computer was an important tool for her, that is all it was—a tool.

Stewart was enthusiastic about Lisa's desire to be at home, but was skeptical about her idea that the computer would be the best cornerstone for a business. He was not impressed when, in the middle of the night, very excited, Lisa shook him awake and blurted out, "Mailing lists!" He couldn't believe anyone would pay her to put together lists of names. He remained unconvinced until Lisa secured her old employer as her first client. From that moment on he was her biggest supporter.

Securing her former employer as a first client gave Lisa the confidence she needed to try to develop a direct mail business. She also offered word processing and data entry services to local companies that were too small to buy their own computers. She began her business with one personal computer, but within six months she added two more PCs and two printers, locating everything in an extra upstairs bedroom that she converted into her office.

Although her new work bore no resemblance to her old job, she threw herself into it with the same devotion. She'd work from nine to five, five days a week, at minimum. At first she took care of her daughter herself, but as her business grew she realized she needed help. Fortunately, her parents lived nearby and were more than willing. Her father had recently retired, so each morning at nine, both her parents would arrive and assume full responsibility for Ellen. Lisa would head upstairs to her office and work until noon, when she'd break for lunch, usually coming downstairs with a bag of laundry in tow. "I put it in while we had lunch, and then I'd take another load back upstairs after lunch." She'd work in her office until five. Stewart's experience with computers was important. He would help out at night and on weekends, taking the information Lisa had gotten from a customer and setting up the necessary computer programs. More often than not, the two of them would work side by side at their computers after Ellen went to bed.

Lisa's family grew as quickly as her business. Within the first full year of business she gave birth to their second child, Jeremy. However, as a self-employed business owner, she had no maternity leave and no backup staff to relieve her of responsibilities. The day she went into labor with Jeremy, she got up at 4:00 A.M. to complete a job that had to be done. When she was being wheeled into the delivery room, she was reminding her husband what clients to call to inform them that their work would be delayed. Two days after the birth, she was able to sit at her computer and finish off a project. For all the benefits of self-employment, there is none of the protective coverage that some employees have, like maternity leave. And running a business is time-consuming.

Although Lisa's home-based business provides immediate and sustained access to her children, it hasn't resulted in radically increasing the blocks of time she spends with them. In fact, she has a constant struggle maintaining some boundaries.

Having a separate office upstairs has helped Lisa in her effforts to keep her work activities separate from her family life. Nonetheless, the two often blur. Her daughter often can't understand why Mommy wants to be left alone.

Sometimes Ellen stands at the door and pounds. There are times I am in the middle of a telephone conversation, and it's just not appropriate to put the receiver down and growl at a two year old. At that time I try to block out what is going on outside and hope the customer doesn't think I am beating someone. Other times I need to go discipline Ellen because she can get out of control. She can work herself up to a fever pitch, and then we've lost the rest of the afternoon. As long as she knows she isn't locked out of my office and she knows she can come and go, she loses interest. The problem comes when she knows the door is locked and she can't come in.

Lisa has tried to make room for Ellen as much as possible in the office, including setting up a miniature work area for her.

My little girl has her own little desk and yellow phone over in the corner of our office. She says she has her own company and she named it after me, "Lisa's company." Sometimes I will get on the telephone and she gets on her yellow phone, and she pretends she is talking to her customers. I have one client, Mr. Matthews, who is a real pain. So she gets on the phone with Mr. Matthews and talks to him all the time.

Despite some of the problems, Lisa believes that she is providing an important role model for her daughter.

Ellen is old enough to be getting a clear picture of what work is and when Mommy has to go to the office. Since she has her own little company, she keeps busy putting labels on envelopes. When she and Grandma are doing that, then she has to come upstairs and get more labels. She is very professional and really self-assured. I don't know if that is just her personality, or the fact that she knows I'm here.

Although her child care arrangement looks ideal, it has some limitations. Lisa realizes that she has to be sure to keep a high profile with her children.

My mother is their grandmother, and there are certain privileges that go with being a grandmother. One of them is that she doesn't like to discipline our children. She doesn't want to overstep her bounds. So sometimes I have to stop work and go discipline them so they know who is in charge. A two year old can't be in charge.

Lisa has tried to keep her operation small—and has, for instance, discouraged clients from coming to her home. But as the business has grown larger new pressures and problems have developed. Periodically she finds it necessary to hire temporary help, which has been difficult. For one thing, she's discovered that some temporary agencies for security reasons don't want to send their workers, mostly female, out to private homes. Once she does manage to get temporary help, it can create chaos. Since her upstairs office is too small for the additional workers, they end up spreading out through the house. For example, one time Lisa was under a tight deadline to send out a mailing. She had three temporary workers, plus her mother, hand-labeling envelopes at the dining room table. Rubber bands and red dots were all over the floor and the baby had to be kept in the living room with the gate up.

Jeremy started screaming—babies know when you are desperate, that's when they start acting up. Then the phone rang in our upstairs office. I went to get it and Ellen came with me. While I was talking to this customer, she knew my defenses were down so she just started slapping labels on the walls and windows. There was enough sun that day to attach them permanently. I still haven't gotten the razor out to take them down.

Despite such difficult moments things seem generally to be working out for the family, but for Lisa the situation has not been without cost. She went from a high profile, socially complex role as a corporate middle manager to working alone on a personal computer in an upstairs bedroom. With the exception of her parents, she lost adult companionship. "There's no one in this neighorhood under fifty. All the younger people are out working." This has been particularly difficult, since she used to depend on her workplace for friendships.

> All my friends were the people at work. When I started working at home, I really missed the adult companionship. It was funny, but all I did was talk about my old company for the first nine months after I left. If someone came over, it was just so natural to get into that conversational pattern of checking out who was doing what and who was responsible for what. It's like an addiction.

Lisa has also lost the luxury of "going home" and leaving the job behind.

> Sometimes when you work in the same place you live, you get the feeling that you never get away. There is a need to get out and get away to break the monotony of being in one place for such long periods of time.

In her worst moments, Lisa even longs for the crowded, dirty commuter bus she used to take to work. Those thirty minutes at least gave her some time alone. Now, as soon as she walks out of the office and down the stairs she's home. Even though she runs a business, being home has also made her feel vulnerable to being stereotyped as "just a homemaker."

> Because I am a woman, people imagine me wearing an apron. I've heard it in people's voices over the telephone, when I tell them my office is at home. They can't understand that I can have a business and not be making cookies or fudge. They see it as the same kind of thing. They don't see professionalism in it. They might see it when the product is generated, but they don't quite understand. I resent it. I don't get this kind of reaction from women who have had children and may have been torn

leaving their children with a baby-sitter. But I do get it from men, even my own brother.

There's also a paradox that Lisa has recognized regarding the whole idea of children and home-based work. She quit her job to be home with her children, but she typically works eight to ten hours a day to make the business a success. It turns out that working at home did not add tremendously to the amount of daytime she spends with her children. Nonetheless, she feels it provides her with immediate access to them in case of an emergency. She is still *there*, even when she is working. When she considers the situation she laughs and says she sometimes worries that her daughter and son will grow up saying that all their mother ever did was work.

The demands of the business have also created some unanticipated strains in her marriage. For one thing, Stewart and Lisa have very little time together in the evening just to relax. "I quit at five sharp, then the evening routine starts. My parents leave, I start dinner, run around and put in the laundry, and Stewart arrives home at six. We eat and put the kids to bed. Then we both go back in the office at 8:30. I usually poop out at 10:30 or 11:00, and he usually works a lot later." For the most part their personal time together consists of working side by side at their computers.

Even though her home-based business has not proven to be ideal in every way, Lisa has decided that it is the best solution for her. She likes being available to her children, and she prefers to be self-employed. She now says that she will probably never return to the corporate world.

Her home-based business has evolved into an entire life-style, one far different than she had ever imagined for herself. She lives and works as part of an extended family—three generations are in her home every day. It seems likely that the business will evolve even further. Stewart is now considering quitting his job with the government and coming into partnership with Lisa. If that happens her home-based work will turn out to have been the cornerstone for a full-fledged family business.

Not all women are lucky enough to have worked out such a satisfying long-term arrangement. For some career women, such as Sara Hegge-Stone, the home-based arrangement will never be anything other than a short-term compromise.

Sara Hegge-Stone

Sara was born toward the tail end of 1944, and like many war babies had a working mother. But unlike others, hers stayed in the work force after the men returned. Sara was the oldest of four children and always aspired to move up and out of her small town environment. At 18 she left for college in California, to major in psychology. She saw a career for herself in child psychology and decided to go on to graduate studies at the University of California at Berkeley.

After her master's degree was completed, Sara took a teaching job at a Boston area private school. She stayed for five years, then accepted a position as the curriculum coordinator for infants and toddlers at a multi-county social service agency. She was responsible for developing teaching programs for emotionally disturbed and mentally retarded toddlers. She loved all aspects of her work: the challenge of developing the most psychologically appropriate programs for these children; the opportunity to work with parents; the team approach used by the agency; the supervision of interns; and her annual salary of $20,000. She was happy and challenged in her work.

In her mid-thirties Sara married Allen, a fellow child psychologist who taught deaf children. They shared many professional interests, as well as the assumption that having a small family would not disrupt Sara's career. When she got pregnant, three years later, she had every intention of returning to work after a short maternity leave. "I never intended to stay home. I thought it would drive me crazy."

But once her son Max was born, Sara, like Lisa, couldn't shake the feeling that she should be the one to raise him. As a psychology graduate student, Sara had taken every infant psychology course available and now became convinced that there were compelling reasons for her to stay home. Her own childhood memories only reinforced this view.

My mother was a grade school teacher and she went back to teaching right after I was born. Different people came in and took care of us kids. Although my mother was available as an educational figure to us, she was not emotionally available. I think that intimacy just made her uncomfortable and so she opted out. I was afraid that if I worked, I would be repeating her pattern.

Sara was determined to provide the emotional and physical presence she had felt deprived of as a child. She also did not want to feel guilty years later for not having stayed home.

I said to myself that ten years from now I might regret it if I hadn't stayed home. I'm not sure, but I think that if I kept up my work and paid somebody else to care for my kids, I would be very sorry when I was fifty or sixty. My husband and I just decided it was worth it for me to stay home and for us to live on his income.

She quit her job with the agency but not without both emotional and financial costs to her and Allen. Their standard of living dropped dramatically—they now had to support three people on $27,000 a year, rather than supporting two on a joint income of $47,000. "It wiped out our savings. It meant me sewing and mending and doing a lot of cooking from scratch, not being able to fix things up, or get things new, or buy the kids much in the way of clothes. We can't take vacations or go out to movies or dinner the way we used to. That kind of stress has been terrible."

In Sara's mind, that stress has never been brought out in the open. From a professional standpoint, she feels that psychologists have been negligent.

> Few experts have any appreciation for the more desperate aspects of what I think women find themselves in. Although more and more women work, it's like a black hole in our culture. I myself feel desperate sometimes, and I'm not sure how much other mothers do, too. Even as close as I have been or as I am to women around here who are working, I'm not sure how much we level with each other about what we give up if we stay home and what we give up if we leave.

What Sara feels she gave up was her sanity. "When I worked I got so much out of it. I liked the adult feeling that I had done a really good day's work and that I was needed and valued. I always worked with teams, and I found them so supportive and rewarding. Being at home now doesn't touch those feelings—in terms of just me."

Sara's loss of a professional identity was compounded by having to assume a home identity as a homemaker—a role she is not completely comfortable with. "When it comes right down to it I am not a good home person. Although I love to cook, I have never liked the grind. I just don't like housework. I find it very hard to get gratification out of being a homemaker. I just don't. I don't get daily feedback from taking care of the house, or cooking, or cleaning."

It came to the point where Sara knew that she had to do something for her own well-being. When Max was eight months old, she decided to look for some type of work outside the home. She wanted a part-time job that would draw on her professional training and that would allow her to continue to nurse Max. It's not surprising that she found herself working in child care.

> I always have been interested in day-care. I found out that a day-care center was starting in Brookline and that the woman had high goals in mind. She was starting an infant program and hired

me as her assistant director. I took Max with me. I liked the job, and it would have worked except that Max kept getting ear infections and had to stay home. So, there I was paying a sitter for him at home and working away from him. It was a zoo. After a few months, I quit. Then I got pregnant with our daughter Megan and didn't try to work again until after I had had her.

Shortly after Megan's birth, the family moved to Southern Florida. Sara and three other neighborhood women began a casual afternoon play group which met in their homes on a rotating basis. Circumstances changed unexpectedly and Sara suddenly found herself running the group full-time.

We hadn't had the play group too long when the marriage of one of the mothers broke up. She immediately had to work full-time, because she was the sole support of her family. She was going to put her kids into day-care. I knew about the local day-care centers and I knew they weren't good. They *really* weren't good; they weren't even okay. By then we all had become attached to each other. And I had started thinking about doing a morning program here at home, because I realized that I wasn't going to get very far from home, since Max kept getting sick. So I said, "I'll take your kids for a limited amount of time." I kept her kids all day for almost eight months and it was exhausting. After that I tried to figure out what I wanted to do next.

Basically she wanted more adult contact and work that drew on skills untapped by running the play group.

I wanted to develop a kind of clearinghouse, where I would track all of the possibilities and alternatives for child care in the area and match them up with the parents' needs. The main stumbling block to this is that most people who care for children don't advertise, because most don't declare their income. It's a very quiet arrangement that they have and they are not about to be listed.

When she realized that a great deal of family day-care is part of the "underground economy," Sara knew that she could not develop a high profile clearinghouse. So she went back to the notion of running her own fee-paying play school in her home. In the process of developing her school she began to discover why so many family day-care providers were not licensed.

I tried to get licensed and fell into a catch-22. I was told if I take two or more children for all day I needed a license, but if I take more than two children for less than three hours and they don't sleep here, then I don't have to be licensed. So I didn't need one. But I still could get closed down because of zoning laws. I checked them through, and a good friend of mine on the city council just told me to lay low. So I am just laying low.

In Sara's mind a morning play school was the most pragmatic transitional solution to the needs of her family. "The play school sort of fit in as the easiest thing for me to do for now. It meets the most needs. It doesn't take my attention away from the kids. I can buy lots of materials and books for the kids, and then write off the stuff that I use."

Although this arrangement works for Sara, it has not been without its problems. On the surface, child care appeals to many mothers because it appears to work so well with their desire to stay home and raise their children. But the realities of running child care as a business are complex, as Sara learned.

From the street Sara's home looked like any other on the tree-shaded cul-de-sac. The large, two-story stucco house sits back from the street, surrounded by a large fenced yard. Evidence of children abound—trikes are in the front yard; drawings are plastered to the door of their large screened-in porch; children's music can be heard. Once inside the front door it is clear the extent to which the home is devoted to children.

To provide the best play-school environment, Sara and Allen completely redesigned their first floor. The living and dining rooms are entirely scaled down to child size. The coat racks stand only three feet high, the shelving goes only as high as an adult knee, and the table and chairs are less than two feet off the ground. There is no adult-sized furniture on their first floor. While most types of home-based work take up a minimum of space or at least can be relegated to a specific room, Sara's child care business has engulfed the entire home. "It would be a lot easier if my work were just in an office here at home—you know, a one-room office. But with kids, they are just all over the place. If we cook, everyone goes in the kitchen. If it rains, there are muddy boots all over. It'd be nice to have a separate part of the house just for the school."

Although child care initially seemed to be an appealing way to earn money and keep a child-centered life-style, it has evolved into a relatively disruptive force in Sara's family. It has precipitated some emotional conflicts for her children. Sara found that they became jealous and competitive; they could not understand why their mother would give so much attention to other children. They would pick fights, throw tantrums, and be uncooperative—all attempts to get her attention. Although her professional skills were challenged by the situation, Sara's emotional energies were drained.

Despite these difficulties Sara has accepted the play school as the best of available alternatives—at least for the short run.

It is working for us right now, but it's hard. It has torn up the floor. It means every morning by nine o'clock, I have to have everything set up and ready to go. It means that I never get away from the kids or the house. But the alternatives would be more difficult for us right now—getting a baby-sitter in or dropping the kids off. This has allowed us to put the kids' needs first, and our feeling is that it has been worth whatever trouble we have had.

Yet, Sara has no intention of staying in the child care business any longer than necessary. "If I feel that Megan is ready, I might get a job outside when she's four. She's two now, so next year she'll have her first year of nursery school, and I'll probably run this school one year more, while she is in nursery school." At which point Sara intends to look for a job that will allow her to extend or develop her skills, and which will put her in more regular contact with adults.

I still would like to get into referrals, matching parents with child care. I think I would be really good at that; I might also look into teaching kids Spanish. I speak Spanish fluently, and they're starting a Spanish program at one of the elementary schools, so I might try to get into that. That excites me because I never taught Spanish to children, so I am starting to look into other things.

Both child care referral and teaching are child-oriented and can be structured around her own children's school days. Sara no longer talks about returning to a full-time position as social service administrator. She is talking about teaching, one of the few jobs that completely coincides with the rhythms and rituals of grade school children. She'd be finished shortly after 3:00 P.M. and would have summers off.

In effect, Sara has terminated her main career as a social service administrator but has found a way to continue a subcareer related to child care. When she considers future job options, she continues to think more in terms of her children and their schedules than she does of advancement in the main career that she pursued until she first gave birth at 37. Although she feels she made the best of a difficult situation she is not entirely at peace with herself.

Unlike the women in the prior chapter who experienced stress and strain in their relationships with their husbands over their decisions to work at home, Sara and the women in this chapter are more likely to feel the stress and strain internally. Sara spoke repeatedly of the desperate struggle she felt in her decision to work or not to work. In effect, she grapples with her own sense of self and her ability to make her own needs equal to or greater than what she perceives to be the needs of her children. It is a struggle in which Sara feels she is not alone.

I have met only one woman who felt that she was doing exactly what she wanted and felt that everybody benefited. No other woman I know, including myself, has had that kind of security. The rest of us are under a lot of stress. I am. And you can go next door to my good friend who decided to work outside, and she is as full of self-doubt about doing it her way.

That kind of self-doubt is not uncommon among women who were raised by traditional women but who spent years pursuing their own careers. Their childhood memories often conflict with career aspirations.

Kindra McClain

After college, Kindra became a free-lance bookkeeper with an odd assortment of clients, who generally did not want to take her financial advice. After several emotionally and financially precarious years, Kindra took a stable bookkeeping job with a leading New York City investment banking firm. She quickly saw opportunities; they quickly saw talent. They paid for her education toward an M.B.A., and she moved into investment banking. When she was in her mid-thirties she met and married Russell, who worked in advertising and was delighted to be marrying a strong, ambitious woman. Their joint income provided for a comfortable life-style, since Kindra earned $150,000 annually, plus bonuses, and Russell earned $60,000.

When she became pregnant at 33, Kindra never questioned how she'd combine work and family.

I always assumed I would continue working. I certainly never imagined staying home full-time with children. I assumed that we would both keep our careers and would hire a housekeeper and nanny. That is what career couples do.

Yet, like Lisa and Sara, Kindra discovered stray and unexpected emotions during her pregnancy. Despite all her prior beliefs, she and her husband found themselves questioning their plans.

I found I was upset all of the time. When the baby was on the way, we had to rethink how we were going to handle it. We could not face both of us working and having someone else at home with the baby all day. I think you get someone else's child at the end of that process. That led us to decide that one of us would have to stay home.

Kindra felt she'd be shirking her moral responsibilities as mother if she allowed anyone else, including her husband, to spend hours each day with her child. It made no difference how well trained or loving that person would be. "I don't care what kind of wonderful British-trained nanny you can find. I think you get somebody else's child at the end of six or ten years. I wanted to be here to train my child my way and give her my ideas and values."

Unlike the traditional woman who assumes automatically that she'll be the one to stay home, Kindra toyed with the possibility that Russell might be the primary nurturer. But the nature of Kindra's job circumstances played a role in the choice they made.

My decision was helped by having things so hectic at work. I got pregnant in May of 1983, and by October, everything was hectic. My boss had been fired. Things were in total chaos. It was clear to me that there was no future for me with the company. I was safe for awhile because they didn't want to be accused of firing a seven-months-pregnant employee, but I knew I wasn't going to have an awful big chance of getting hired by anyone else. I didn't have a lot of options. Since I was so very unhappy with the atmosphere at work, I decided I would be the one to stay home. My husband loved his job and, to be honest, we never seriously discussed him staying home.

The legacy of the traditional marriage contract lingered in Kindra's thoughts and decisions. Not only did she feel no one else would be as well qualified to take care of the baby, she also used her child to help her leave an unhappy job situation. Once her child was born, she never considered searching for another position. In her mind, she either had to find a job while she was pregnant or she wouldn't do it at all. In an unspoken way Kindra wanted the traditional terms of marriage: Russell would be the breadwinner and she the mother at home.

But her desires also forced a radical change in their style of life. With a combined income of over $200,000 they lived a good life in Manhattan. "I was a city girl. I was always jumping in a cab and going anywhere—to the opera, to the museums, to a nice restaurant here, a movie there. I never learned to drive; I didn't need to." But once she stopped working they were forced to live on $60,000 —good money in most parts of the United States, but not New York City. They decided they had to move out of Manhattan because they could not afford the quality of life they wanted, either for themselves or their child. Good housing was impossible. A two-bedroom apartment in the kind of neighborhood where they wanted to live would easily cost them over a quarter of a million dollars. What's more, they were not convinced that the city or even the surrounding suburbs supported the values they wanted to instill in their children. Kindra summarily dismissed Long Island, the area most convenient to where her husband worked. "I think that the people that move out there tend to be the grasping end of the middle class. The values they transmit to their kids are not the ones I want my kids exposed to."

Kindra's reactions were forged in large measure as a reaction to the rootlessness of her own childhood. Raised in a military family, she had known the pain of constant leave-taking. In contrast to her experiences, she wanted her children to have a sense of community. She looked at various possible communities to try to find one that to her most nearly embodied the values she wanted her children to have. While Long Island failed the test, the small New England towns in the Housatonic Valley in Connecticut seemed perfect. Kindra had very strong images of small town life.

> In little towns, everybody knows all their neighbors. They all take care of each other. They place a big emphasis on family, the school, the church. They create environments in which children can be in control—they can walk to school; they can go where they want; they know enough adults so that they don't have to feel threatened. They don't have to be supervised as much.

Once they had focused on the area Kindra and Russell spent several months searching for a home in the Valley. They kept returning to Sharon, a small community about ninety miles from New York. One Sunday, when Kindra was seven months pregnant, they came across a house that entirely suited their dreams, which had just gone on the market. A sprawling, five-bedroom Victorian home with a wraparound front porch, it was only a block from the central village green. Although the house was idyllic, the commute for Russell would not be. He would have to drive four hours a day, to and from his job. He was willing to do it.

Over the next two months they set their dream in motion. On the December day Kindra was released from the hospital with their infant son, Benjamin, their family moved from New York City, population seven million, to Sharon, with a population of three thousand.

For Kindra, the changes were dramatic and immediate. She went from being a Wall Street banker to being unemployed; from being an experienced Manhattanite to being a citizen of a country town; from being a veteran cab rider to being a pedestrian in a place with no public transportation. Most important, she went from being a career woman with no children to being the unemployed mother of an infant.

Kindra found herself at home alone with a new baby, living in a community in which she knew no one and had no driver's license. As much as she loved her son, the company of an infant was not enough to satisfy her.

The transition to one income also proved difficult. Even with the savings she had from her Wall Street days, the costs of repairing their old Victorian house exceeded what they could afford. Just as important, Kindra missed working; she missed the sense of direction and discipline it gave her. She found herself getting up in the morning with barely enough energy to get through the day. She procrastinated and took forever to do projects that she would have quickly whipped off in spare moments back in her hectic New York days. Although she felt good about being with her son, her own listlessness depressed her and she decided she had to get back on some type of work track. A home-based business seemed to offer the best solution to her competing desires to be home and to work.

Drawing on the bookkeeping skills she had developed back before she'd gone into investment banking, Kindra decided to buy a personal computer and do free-lance bookkeeping for local businesses. She bought the necessary equipment, set up a front room of the house as an office, and hired a housekeeper to come in two days a week, freeing her from the daily grind of housework. She also arranged for several neighborhood girls to come in after school and take care of her son for several hours so she would have blocks of uninterrupted time to work. She began circulating flyers and advertising weekly in the local newspapers.

Kindra applied all her organizational skills to the task of starting a business, convinced that all she had to do was "open the doors and advertise." Wrong. In the first year she grossed less than $1000— quite a shock for a woman who used to gross over $150,000 a year. She was shaken by the experience.

Kindra had assumed that she could readily translate her success on Wall Street to success on Main Street, USA. She'd failed to recognize that in a small town she needed a very different approach to marketing a new business, especially since she was a newcomer to the community.

Rather than spending time getting to know people and to becoming friendly with them, she had relied on marketing techniques like flyers. This would have been more appropriate to a larger city, where face-to-face recognition and community standing play a smaller role in business.

What is curious about Kindra's situation—as with Lisa Jacobi's —is that despite her success and experience in the business world she possessed little of the savvy or confidence needed to start her own business. Although counted among "New woman business owners" in Small Business Administration statistics, neither Lisa nor Kindra had the typical psychological profile, capital, or business vision characteristic of entrepreneurs. They became business owners by default, backing into it as a solution, rather than pursuing it as an ambition. It is worth considering that what has euphemistically and optimistically been hailed as the "era of the female entrepreneur" may be in large part the result of career mothers being torn between work and family and accepting self-employment as their only real option. In Kindra's case, getting her business going required a tremendous effort, as she had to figure it out as she went along.

After a year of struggling and a growing sense of failure, compounded by sheer loneliness, Kindra began to focus on the inequity of the bargain she had struck with her husband.

Fatherhood is really only a weekend job for him. He is not home with our son all the time, so it hasn't been such a great change for him. And it was easier for him to sever ties with New York, because he had only lived there for four years. I lived there for over fifteen. It's been hard to move up here. I now have to drive and I hate the prospect, but I know that it's really a necessity in order to survive up here. That has been the thorn in my side.

She admits that he has a long commute, but justifies it on the grounds that he loves to drive. Kindra feels that she has had to absorb virtually the whole impact of motherhood and making the transition to Sharon. Their entire move had been set in motion by the feelings and ideas about motherhood that she had not been aware of until her pregnancy. Once she set those beliefs into action—quitting her job, moving to a small town—she experienced the practical consequences and found herself unprepared.

Kindra's belief that she as a mother should stay home limited her options regarding her career. Her idea that small towns would offer a better environment for her family took her right out of the lifestyle she had chosen for herself as an adult. Although she has achieved what she thought she wanted, she has found that her new life-style is not without its own problems. She is alone, with a new baby, a struggling business, and no driver's license, living in a community that is ninety miles from her closest friend. For her the conflict between work and family has yet to be resolved.

Anne Slade

Anne lives in San Francisco with her husband, Peter, and two daughters ages five and eight. Her husband earns over $100,000 a year with a major insurance company. They own a cabin on the north coast, a sailboat docked on the bay, and a lovely, three-story house in Pacific Heights with a view of the Golden Gate Bridge. They travel a great deal—a two-week vacation in Mexico and a trip abroad every year.

A tousle-haired brunette, Anne was born and raised on the East Coast. She went to the University of Connecticut for her bachelor's degree and went on to get her master's degree in health administration in California. To her delight, she landed a plum position as the assistant director of a major university hospital in San Francisco. She traveled extensively for her job and enjoyed her work immensely.

Even with all this she "just assumed" she would quit when she got pregnant at 30. "Since we didn't need my income, my husband and I decided that one of us should be home to raise the children. He had more income, so therefore we decided that I would stay home."

From 1979 to 1984, Anne did not pursue any paying job and

concentrated all her energies on her two daughters, born sixteen months apart. She found it quite a contrast to her executive days. "It was hard at home the first year or two, because I had no control over my situation. The kids were in control. That was real hard because I was used to being in control."

As her children got older, she began channeling her energies into their schools, her family activities, and her friends. She served as president of the parents' organization, and as room mother for their parties and class activities. She organized the family weekend trips to the cabin or on their sailboat. She served as the "glue that kept all of our friends and our friends' network together. I was the one who would call everybody and make plans for us all together." She stressed that during those four or five years they had an extremely active family life and that she liked being able to organize and enjoy the family activities.

Anne thought that she had lost her desire to work for pay, subordinating it to her desire to work for her family and school activities. But once she started to get a paycheck again, she found herself hooked.

In 1983 Anne and a neighbor, Leslie, made Christmas wreaths out of pine cones as presents for friends. As "a lark" the next year, they decided to make some more and sell them to stores. They wanted to go for "quality stores"—their wreaths were finely detailed, high quality items. To their delight such exclusive department stores as Neiman Marcus and Saks Fifth Avenue immediately bought their products. What began as an impulse quickly became a labor intensive business, in which Anne and Leslie worked fifty to sixty hours a week during the holiday rush. Although they never drew up a formal partnership agreement, they kept running records of their expenses, paying out of their husbands' accounts since "We really didn't have money of our own, per se." Anne just assumed that after expenses they would divvy up the profits evenly, fifty-fifty. Unlike most crafts businesses that have a difficult time turning a profit, theirs netted over $10,000 the first year.

The business promised to do well even beyond the Christmas

season, so Anne prepared for a long work schedule. She set up a workbench in her basement and spent a lot of her time there, arranging and constructing wreaths. In the evenings, she'd sometimes haul her materials up to the kitchen table, so she could be around her kids, but the smell and stickiness of the glue made it an unpleasant experience for everyone.

The most gratifying part for Anne came from her increased sense of self-esteem: "Women who work have a lot more stature in our society than women who stay home with their children. I felt superior to other women who didn't work. I'd meet them at parties and they were very interested in what I did; they were almost envious. I felt like I had achieved something they had not achieved."

She also felt that she was treated differently by her husband's colleagues once she started her business.

> Before I started our crafts business there were very few men who would give me a second thought if they thought I didn't work. But once I started my business I was more than just my husband's wife. Recently my husband had an open house in his office. Everybody had their name tags on. Under my name they wrote "Independent Business Owner." I got a lot of people coming up saying "Oh, what do you do?" and I would say, "I have a home-based business." You know, I didn't have to say "I am his wife."

As the business got bigger and more demanding, Anne began to have to make decisions that subordinated her family needs to the needs of her business. She was not able to have dinner ready every evening; she was not able to take a business trip with her husband; she had to forgo a school meeting. These decisions precipitated a real conflict in her, which was exacerbated when her husband told her she was "driven." She felt increasingly guilty that her family was being deprived of the wife and mother they had bargained for. She felt she was shirking the responsibilities she assumed when she became a full-time wife and mother. In addition to the strain that the work was causing in her family, a year of unspoken grudges with her business partner precipitated a crisis in their relationship.

Anne had begun to work forty-hour weeks, longer hours than she wanted. Yet her partner, who had an M.B.A. and great plans for the business, felt that Anne was not working enough. Both felt increasing resentment that came out in the open when at the end of the first year of business Leslie handed Anne a ten-page typed financial statement, specifying that Anne would get 30 percent of the profits, while Leslie would get 70 percent on the basis of work done. Anne was stunned.

> We were really like sisters and for her to do something like that was a shock. I was too hurt to fight with her, so I agreed to give her most of the money. The business was more of a power trip for her than it was for me. I enjoyed the self-fulfillment of creating something, selling, and getting the feedback. I wasn't going to argue with her—it wasn't worth it to me.

The thought that Leslie would maximize her own interests at Anne's expense hurt her deeply. It was really a shock to realize that Leslie saw their partnership as a business transaction rather than the almost familial relationship Anne had envisioned it would be. She had entered the arrangement as "a lark" and simply had no sense of how to fight for her share.

Only later did her anger at the inequity of the split surface through the hurt. Then she regretted that they had never had a partnership agreement specifying terms regarding hours worked and splitting the profits.

Though she loved working, the combination of the strained partnership and her own conflict between family and job forced Anne to quit the business, but not without regret.

> You know I already miss the work. Once you step away from work and you don't touch it all—like I did right after the children

were born—it's okay. So long as I didn't touch it or get my hands on it I was okay. But once I started working again, I got all of these feelings back. I began to feel like I was okay again. Now I sometimes feel like a ditch digger without a shovel.

The career women in this chapter were surprised at the intense new feelings they experienced during their pregnancies. They knew they would love their children, but were unprepared for some of the feelings having children released—especially the vivid memories of their own childhood. They discovered that their feelings and expectations about themselves as mothers were rooted in their own experiences as children. Most of them had been raised by full-time homemakers whose examples set the standards for what a good mother should do.

Lisa, Sara, Kindra, and Anne ended up feeling that they had to choose between their careers and their children—between the working women they were and the mothers they wanted to be. This is a "choice" their husbands did not have to make and couldn't fully grasp. They were not raised to think about changing their career plans to be "good fathers." As a result, the choice the women have to make is a burden, since neither option is satisfactory—and the quality of their children's lives seems to hang in the balance. These women tell of desperation, conflict, fear, and intense anxiety as to whether they are doing the right thing—*whatever* they choose to do.

As we have seen, working at home is frequently seen as the best compromise solution. Since few employers allow their employees to work entirely from home, most women have to quit their jobs and stop being employees with clearly defined advancement paths. They relinquish tangible measures of success such as promotions and titles, as well as social contact and feedback from peers. They reduce or lose their paychecks, which affects their self-esteem and often their relationships with their husbands. Moreover, starting a business is not easy. If one is to succeed, a new business requires long hours, and most women find they need help with child care.

Some skills don't convert easily into use in a home-based business—it requires a great deal of knowledge, confidence, and savvy. Although a home-based business is certainly an option for career women who want to be mothers it can't be promoted as "the answer."

4

Homemakers and Career Women in Family Businesses

The American family has changed drastically. The traditional notion of family in which the father goes to work and the mother stays home is undergoing profound change, as more women work and nearly one out of every two marriages end in divorce. New family configurations are emerging. Single-parent households, most often headed by women, are common. There are blended families and families linked to each other as a result of divorce and remarriage: stepchildren, ex-spouses, in-laws, and ex-in-laws must find ways to live and interact in peace. Most two-parent households now need two incomes leading to unanticipated stress as parents try to combine work and family.

Experts from all sides—the right and the left, conservative and liberal—insist that efforts be made to alleviate this strain and strengthen the family. They often call for a renewal of traditional values and emphasize closer bonds and working together for common goals. Within this context family businesses are often promoted as a solution for the problems faced by families—by living and working together, traditional values can be renewed and families strengthened. In the early 1980s, Congressman Newt Gingrich introduced the Family Opportunity Act into the United States Congress. If approved (which it wasn't), this national legislation would have granted tax incentives for home computers to encourage families to learn and earn together at home. The emphasis was entirely on the technology as if this would be the common bond behind any kind of family business. This kind of effort implies that all family businesses are cut from the same cloth, all started for the same reasons, all capable of accomplishing the same goals. They are not.

There is not one kind of family business, any more than there is one kind of working woman. Different types of family businesses are started for different reasons, serve different purposes, and result in different degrees of emotional and financial satisfaction for the men and women in them. Some couples experience joy and gratification and are brought closer together by their efforts; others find frustration and claustrophobia and are strained by the competing demands of business and family.

Some family businesses work and some don't, and the reasons why are complicated and not well understood. In 1985, the Small Business Administration of the federal government estimated that there were over 13 million family businesses in the United States. Yet they could reveal little about them, much less the ties between the structure of the business and the structure of the family. Just as families change so does the relationship between the business and the family. Traditional marriages result in different types of family businesses from partnership marriages, and the changes that have affected the relationships of men and women in general have affected couples that run family businesses.

Noreen Holman

Born in Milwaukee in 1948, Noreen grew up believing that her major goal should be to "marry right." As a young woman, she thought of career in terms of a husband's success, not her own. During her junior year in college she met Eric Holman. His lean good looks and his intense ambition attracted her. She liked the idea of being married to a potentially wealthy and powerful man. When he graduated the following summer, she willingly left her Midwestern college, ten credits short of graduation, to move to San Francisco, where he took a job with a major West Coast bank. They married shortly thereafter and she took a job as a receptionist with a top commercial photographer.

The job developed to where she worked as his stylist. Although the studio was prestigious, her job was not. "I had to run all over the city, making sure that every detail was perfect for a picture—the costumes had to be right; the make-up artist had to be just so; and the hairdresser had to be perfect. It was just incredible busywork; the amount of creativity required was pretty low. I was really just executing someone else's ideas and I hated it."

Noreen's abilities clearly exceeded the demands of her job, but she did not have the education or training necessary to land a job that would challenge her. Like many traditional women, she found herself with no clear career options, partially a result of her decision to forgo a college degree.

"I didn't know what I wanted to do next with my life. I think a woman reaches a point in her working life when she's not happy but not quite sure what she wants to do. She says, 'This might be a perfect opportunity to have a baby.' That's what I did. I had Lauren." Given her traditional values, Noreen's decision was logical. Moving on to motherhood provided a solution and gave her direction. Two years later she gave birth to Peter.

For several years Noreen was content. Motherhood was both new and exhausting and she had little time to ponder what else she might like to do. By the time Lauren was ready for nursery school, Noreen found she wanted more for herself. "Although I loved being with the children, I missed talking to adults, and I missed the contact with the outside world. I started getting a little antsy."

By then Eric was as restless as Noreen. Both had accomplished major goals—Noreen had given birth to two beautiful children and Eric was a vice-president of one of the top banks on the West

Coast—yet neither was satisfied. Noreen wanted to do something in addition to being a mother, and Eric no longer wanted to work for someone else.

Eric was convinced that there was an entirely untapped market for gourmet foods and gourmet cooking equipment. Although people were increasingly interested in cooking, they found it difficult to locate the right ingredients and tools. Eric decided to start his own company to design and manufacture cooking utensils and to distribute gourmet foodstuffs on a retail basis in his San Francisco stores as well as on a mail-order basis. His plan provided an ideal opportunity for Noreen. "I thought Eric's business would be the perfect opportunity for me to get involved in something besides my children."

It was a fortuitous combination of convenience, accessibility, and happenstance. She could stay home with Lauren and Peter, try her hand at something that interested her, and draw on her experience as a wife and cook. Like many traditional women, Noreen's decision to work in a family business was the result more of circumstances than of her deliberate calculated initiative.

Noreen began by designing the package labels for Eric's products, developing their names and writing the catchy phrases that would hold a shopper's eye. From there she went on to write the copy for their ads in food magazines. She discovered that she not only loved the work but was very good at it. Eric was always being complimented on the copy she wrote—although few people in the business world had any idea she was the one responsible for it.

The company was successful, and it was Eric's pride and joy. For years he never told anyone that Noreen had anything to do with it.

At first, it didn't particularly bother me, but later on it started to get to me. I remember that we had a sales meeting where all of our sales representatives came to hear about plans for the coming year and to be congratulated or scolded for their work. My husband thanked a number of the people in the room who had contributed to various things. When it was over, I noticed that he had not bothered to even mention that I was involved. After the meeting, I asked him why he didn't say anything and he said, "Gosh, I'm sorry. I just didn't think about it." From that point on, he started telling people. It was as though it had never occurred to him to tell anyone or to mention it. Or maybe he didn't want to. I don't know. I prefer not to think about it.

Like most women, Noreen preferred to leave areas of her relationship unexplored, preferring the ambiguity of not knowing to the certainty of knowing something that would disappoint or be difficult. Eric's not acknowledging her work role reflected decisions they had made about their roles in the family and the business.

Eric assumed the high-profile, public side of the business while Noreen worked in a low-profile, behind-the-scenes manner. Eric commuted to their San Francisco offices while Noreen worked in their Marin County home to be near their children. Eric was the company's president and chief executive officer. Noreen had no title. Eric received a regular paycheck, Noreen was not paid. Their roles in the company were logical extensions of their traditional roles in the family. As the breadwinner, Eric took charge of the public domain of work and earned enough to support his family. As wife and mother, Noreen helped him out in his business, but was primarily "at home with our kids." According to this arrangement she didn't need to be paid so long as he supported her properly.

Once Noreen recognized these terms and realized that she didn't like them, she also began to question some of the fundamental attitudes that had shaped her life.

I became much more aware of my own needs and realized that there were things that I wanted to accomplish for myself. While I do things for Eric and I try to live up to what he wants in a wife, I don't want to make my needs secondary to his. With maturity I have learned that I need to fulfill myself and be happy with myself.

Noreen may feel confident about placing her needs as equal to or above those of her husband, but she does not make that claim regarding her children. "Taking care of my children in a responsible fashion is the most important thing in my life. In my priorities it is children, self, and husband—in that order. But children and self are very tied together for women. They are very hard to separate."

Sandwiched between children and husband, Noreen has competing desires regarding her home-based public relations work. On the one hand she feels that working at home is not good for her relationship with her husband or for her own well-being. On the other hand, she wants to stay with the business because it gives her the chance to work at home and be near her children during the day.

For business reasons Eric and Noreen recently transferred company headquarters from San Francisco to Chicago and settled into a large, three-bedroom apartment. By any measure theirs is a spacious apartment, but with two children there is no longer an extra bedroom in which Noreen can work. The change of circumstances has intensified tensions between Noreen and Eric.

Her desk is now located in their master bedroom and Eric uses it as his dirty clothes hamper. Not only does she dislike having to take his dirty shirts off her desk before she can sit down to work in the morning, she also feels it is evidence of the fact that he does not treat her as a serious co-worker.

Her frustration is compounded by the fact that they continue to work in two places—he in a downtown office and she at home. Because she is "at home" he sometimes seems to forget that she works and he also does not want to discuss business when he comes home. He expects to be greeted by his wife, rather than his company's public relations person. "Many times, I have had to say, 'Look, you asked me to do this work and I have worked eight hours on it today. You have *got* to make some time to talk to me—even if you have to pencil me into your calendar and treat me like an outside account.'"

Noreen is living in a new city, knows no one, and works alone. When Eric comes home in the evening, he is often the first adult she has spoken to all day. She needs to talk business, but she also just needs to talk. She feels isolated, and knows that she must somehow get out of the house in order to feel that she is a credible, serious worker.

> I am people-starved at this point. I think part of the reason that I get up in the morning and take a shower and put on makeup is the need to feel good about myself. I think it would help to have feedback from other people as well. One of the things I really miss is the friendship of men. I have a few close female friends whom I treasure, but I really enjoy the stimulation of talking to men, and men friends are just easier to make in an office situation.

Anyone who works at home complains at one time or another about isolation and loneliness. Noreen has pinpointed a major limitation of the home as workplace—the lack of the opposite sex. Informal interaction and relationships between men and women can harmlessly occur in an office whereas the same benign flirtation or conversation becomes more charged, carries more weight, or may have more serious implications when it occurs outside of work.

Noreen misses those casual exchanges, although her husband is actually delighted that this element is not in her life. "He thinks this arrangement is wonderful—it's so non-threatening to him. He is afraid I am going to develop a whole new set of friends, especially men, and that he won't have anything to do with them."

The question becomes obvious—when there are so many sources of dissatisfaction, why does Noreen continue to work for her husband at home? The answer lies in the sense of priorities. She places her children's needs above her own, and she is convinced they need her to be at home. As they get older she claims that they need her even more than they did before.

Noreen's intense feelings of duty tend to create conflict during any typical workday and explain why she feels that working at home is even more difficult than having an outside job.

If I could close my door at 3:00 P.M. and not come out when my children come home from school, and if my children understood that Mommy is unavailable to them for that period of time, until the time when other mommies come home from the office, then I'd get more work done. But I can't. For example, last week I was working on copy for an ad, and I realized it was time to pick my son up at school. And I said to myself, Should I phone the baby-sitter to do it or should I go myself? And I thought, Gee, I really haven't spent that much time with Pete this week. I have been so busy, maybe I should just go and take a half hour and pick him up at school and let him play in the playground and then I'll come back and then I'll work on my copy some more. So I went to school. But I didn't get back to the ad. If I had been in an office I would have just sat there and finished it.

As Noreen has learned, a mother who works at home has to exercise a great deal more self-discipline than someone who has the support of an organized environment devoted exclusively to work. The workplace has a structure and certain formal rules—regarding the number of hours to work, the times to start and finish, and the ways in which work can and can't be interrupted. This structure and its boundaries help working women separate family and job. They can leave in the morning and come back to it later, but they do not have to try to be mother, wife, and professional at the same time in the same place.

Noreen is angry that people do not recognize the difficulties of working at home, and that many of them make the assumption that it must be an ideal situation, that she has the best of both worlds. "My husband once said to me, 'Why would you even want to work outside the home? Isn't it terrific being able to have such a 'flexible schedule?' Flexible! I have such a wonderfully 'flexible' schedule: I hate that word."

In common public discourse "flexible" seems to have an entirely positive connotation. For someone who works at home, "flexible" is a synonym for "unstructured," "unorganized," and potentially "out of control." The more "flexible" the work situation is, the harder one has to struggle to establish discipline and control. "Flexibility" is in reality a tremendously difficult challenge.

> How do you separate your personal life from your professional life? There's a great overlapping. Tremendous overlapping. It happens constantly. It happens at night, when I find myself under a lot of pressure, using my "free time" because I have done so much running around with the kids during the day. I find myself working at ten or eleven at night, cutting into my time with my husband. If I worked in an office, I'm sure I'd accomplish a great deal more.

Noreen has learned the painful lesson that a flexible work schedule means that she shoulders the sole responsibility for setting the boundaries between her work and her family.

Despite the difficulties, Noreen has enjoyed certain advantages from working in a family business. Although not paid as much as she would like, after five years Noreen did begin to receive a paycheck. In many family businesses, only one paycheck is drawn and it is made out to the man. Although his family's financial needs may be taken care of, his wife's needs—to be recognized and be paid for her labors—are not. Many people, both women and men, can't help linking their sense of independence and part of their sense of self with a paycheck. A woman who helps out her husband in his business often grows frustrated by the sense that hers is a powerless and dependent role. She may seek another job as much out of a desire for independence as out of a desire for money of her own. This is true in Noreen's case.

Because of the nature of their family business Noreen had an opportunity to cultivate professionally marketable skills, and she intends to use them to work somewhere else. Often traditional women who help their husbands assume the clerical work—typing, transcribing, inventorying, or bookkeeping—rather than professional or managerial responsibilities. Although the type of business

Eric started gave Noreen an opportunity in this area it was her own initiative and risk taking—and Eric's receptivity—that led her to take advantage of it. After ten years in the family business Noreen is in a much better position to pursue a career in the outside world than she had been as a photographer's assistant.

Eric is not really enthusiastic about her plan to depart from the business, but Noreen is convinced that the break will come as soon as her children are old enough. She wants more autonomy, creativity, and money than is currently possible within the family business. What keeps her at home at this point are the children's needs, not Eric's expectations for his wife and colleague. Despite the fact that they started out in a traditional marriage and that their business roles reflected that relationship, Noreen and Eric are now open to changing their roles because they are no longer happy in them.

Not all women in traditional marriages and family businesses are so lucky. Rita Wyler, although similar in many ways to Noreen, feels that her marriage and family business are so interwoven that to pull back from the business would destroy the marriage.

Rita Wyler

Eric Holman started his gourmet food products business because he was sick of working for someone else. Paul Wyler started his business in order to re-create the type of family life he had known as a child.

The eldest of seven children, Paul was raised on a small dairy farm in Wisconsin, learning at a young age what hard work meant. Up at five every morning, he finished two hours of chores before he left for school. In the evenings and during harvest, he had even more to do. He came to know his parents through their work and in the process forged his notions of life and women.

After a stint with the army, he went to work for a feed business in upstate New York and dreamed of owning his own farm. He wanted a woman as strong and forceful as his mother had been. He had watched her raise seven children, run the house, handle the books, and drive a tractor, and he expected the woman he married to be capable of the same. He never kidded around with women about his expectations, so when he met Rita in the mid-1960s he let her know exactly where he stood on the issue of women and work. He wanted his wife to work—not for someone else but alongside him.

Rita came from an entirely different background and was less than enthusiastic about many of his expectations. As the executive assistant to the president of an insurance company, she worked with the board of directors and was responsible for writing the annual report. She loved the high-profile, sophisticated life of business and could not envision forfeiting her prospects for a farm. Although she longed to have children, and intended to quit working for the first several years of their lives, she had every intention of getting another job after the children started first grade. Paul was offering her a future quite different from what she had ever considered and she wasn't sure she could be the traditional farm wife and mother he wanted. Yet, he was uncompromising—and she was in love.

Paul and Rita were married in a big church wedding in the fall of 1968. By late 1969, Rita had quit her job with the insurance company and was pregnant with their first child, a daughter. Two years later, she gave birth to their son. When her youngest was seven months old, Paul was offered the opportunity to buy the feed business that he had worked for for years. Although not a farm, it was a step in the right direction.

He desperately wanted it and Rita backed him entirely, although she made her priorities clear. "I said the children would come first, the business second, and the housework, whenever." She was convinced that unless she laid out the terms early on Paul would ultimately re-create the situation he'd grown up in, where the business and its needs would come before everything else. Paul agreed with her terms—at least in principle.

Having arranged the necessary loans, "they" bought the feed business, although in reality Paul owned it, since all of the financial and legal documents were in his name. Because this practice is common in agricultural communities, neither Paul nor Rita questioned it. Nor did Rita initially question the fact that only Paul drew a paycheck from the business. For one thing, the business could only support one paycheck in the early years, and in any case Paul had a very traditional sense of wanting to support his family. What counted was that they thought of it as "their" family business.

Like Noreen and Eric Holman, Paul and Rita Wyler established the "alone-together" type of family business. Paul spent his days at the feed center ten miles from their home, and Rita worked alone at home, handling the office work. They have continued this arrangement for the fifteen years they have owned and operated the feed business. Paul handles the sales and technical end of the business while Rita does the behind-the-scenes work of bookkeeping, billing, and payroll at home. She also takes all of the business calls on their home phone.

Although Paul would have preferred that they work side by side, day by day, such an arrangement was impossible. Obviously they could not move the feed center to their home, and neither of them wanted Rita to move the office to the feed center and leave the children in the care of someone else. They agreed that her first responsibility was to be at home raising them.

At the beginning, Rita was delighted at the chance to do the phone and paperwork for the business. She set up her office in a spare room in their basement but quickly discovered that with two young children her life revolved around the kitchen, not the basement. After six months of running up and down the stairs constantly, she transferred her work to the kitchen and started taking calls on their kitchen phone.

Although the arrangement was good in certain ways, it had drawbacks. She lost any physical separation between the work and the family. The kitchen became the hub of both the family and the business and there was often competition between them. The kids had to learn early on when the phone rang they were supposed to be quiet. They frequently defied this rule—largely, Rita thinks, because they were jealous she was giving so much of her attention to the job. "As soon as the phone would ring, they would start to scream. Sometimes they were so bad I had to walk out onto the patio in the snow just to be able to handle a call. There was no other way to do it. When they were little, I really couldn't do anything once they started to scream."

Rita often felt that she was a prisoner of the phone, because she always had to stay home to take the calls. Eventually they bought a phone-answering machine so she could be free to take the children places and to run errands during the day, but the machine did not solve all their problems. "People call us at six in the morning or eleven at night. Since I don't know a thing about livestock or feed, they have to call Paul before he goes out in the morning or after he comes back at night."

Paul appears oblivious to the constant ringing of the phone or the fact that the paperwork ends up all over the house. On the contrary, he takes pleasure in having the work so accessible. Since he is consumed by his business, he likes being able to work whenever he feels like it. Although he agreed in principle to Rita's initial demands that family come first, in reality he has never known that type of situation. People are creatures of habit, and by habit business always came first in his life.

Rita, on the other hand, didn't grow up in that kind of environment and she feels invaded and deprived. Since the office is all over the house, she feels she has no home to come to. When her children were young, particularly before they started school, she accepted the situation because her primary responsibility was to be home to raise them. "I felt that working at home was the only way I could work. I didn't feel like I had many options." But she also enjoyed the work more then. "Everything in the business was new. We had to start everything from scratch, so it was a challenge and it was kind of fun."

As her daughter and son got older and the newness wore off,

Rita was no longer so content. "I like to work to the best of my abilities. I like to be challenged and I like to be able to measure my abilities. I need to be rewarded emotionally and financially. The work that I do now doesn't do that. It is very, very simple and just not challenging. I can do much more than I am doing."

Rita would like the type of feedback a person gets when they have a job working with other people. She'd also like a paycheck. At first it didn't bother her that she was not paid for her clerical work for the feed business, but after a while she found she wanted both money and recognition. "It's very hard to pat yourself on the back. And there is nobody here to do that. You miss having a mirror of how you are doing and what you are. It's very easy to lose perspective when you work alone and have the telephone as your only connection with the outside world."

Despite her desire to pursue more challenging work, Rita is ambivalent and uncertain about what to do. Ideally, she would like to work full-time outside the home doing the kind of work that she did before she got married—but feels she can't. She is afraid she'd end up feeling like a failure for not giving proper attention either to her husband and children or the job. She doesn't feel she has enough energy to take on a full-time job in addition to all of her responsibilities at home. Most important, she's afraid that if she quit her office work, she'd jeopardize her marriage.

Paul would not be happy if Rita left the family business to work elsewhere. His attitude toward a working wife has not changed in the nearly twenty years they've been married. "He's opposed to my working outside the home and absolutely in favor of my working for his business."

"His business" has become the core of their life and Rita is afraid that if they couldn't talk about the business, they would have nothing else to talk about. She also fears that if she relinquishes the office work, she would relinquish some of her power and influence in the marriage. "I like to know what's going on all the time. I like to have something to say about things, and I can't have anything to say about things if I don't understand what's going on."

As a result, Rita recently decided that if she wanted a job outside the home, it would have to be in addition to, rather than instead of, her work for the feed business. Most of the part-time jobs available, such as being a salesclerk in a local shopping mall, were utterly unappealing. They paid too little and provided little challenge. Ultimately she decided to get her real estate license, feeling this would provide the best compromise among her competing desires. "Selling real estate would be an independent type of job where I could do as much as I wanted, and go as far as I chose to go. And it would be flexible so that I could still do the office work for Paul at home."

Paul truly was baffled by Rita's desire. He simply could not understand why she wanted another job. He felt that her needs should be satisfied by her work with the feed business and the family. Like most traditional men, he equated work with money, and since he earned enough to support his family comfortably, he saw no reason why Rita would want to work. He came to accept her desire as a whim to be tolerated and treated it accordingly, which meant, among other things, that he didn't take her efforts to get a real estate license seriously. "I missed many classes because Paul would schedule meetings for the same nights I had classes; it just never entered his mind that I had class every Tuesday and Thursday. Every day I'd remind him, but he'd still forget." He also saw no need to help out with the cooking and cleaning, since he felt that she didn't *have* to work and that if she *wanted* to work it was fine so long as it didn't interfere with her duties for the feed business or family.

As a result, Rita now has a huge workload and multiple roles— wife, mother, homemaker, secretary for the feed business, and real estate agent. Her work schedule is daunting. She spends twenty-five hours a week selling real estate, twenty hours a week doing the secretarial work for the business, and countless hours cooking, cleaning, shopping, and coordinating a household that includes two active teenagers. Yet she feels that this arrangement is easier than a conventional nine-to-five job. Her real estate work is flexible and can be scheduled to accommodate the shifting demands of the feed business, her children, and husband.

Over the years Rita says that she has learned to schedule what she wants to do in a time frame that does not interfere with or inhibit anyone else's needs.

> All the women I know say the same thing—their needs are considered, even by themselves, to be of less importance than anyone else's in the family. It's not a martyr thing, it is just the one thing that you have control over. You control your own needs. You cannot control the other people and what they want and need. All of my friends feel badly about the fact that what they want is at the bottom of the list.

Twenty years after her wedding Rita finds herself with the same conflicts she experienced when she first met Paul. How does she help Paul achieve his dreams, keep their family together, and yet satisfy her own needs? Like many women, Rita resolved these conflicts by exercising the only control she has—over how and when she meets her own needs, and she often subordinates these. Unlike Noreen, who challenged that notion, Rita still lives by it, although unhappily so.

Rita's notion of the ideal way to balance the various aspects of her life reveals a woman struggling with the traditional terms of marriage.

> Ideally, I would work at an extremely challenging and stimulating job from nine to three every day. I'd have a housekeeper, because I can't be bothered to cook or clean. And I would split the responsibilities for the children fifty-fifty. When I talk about that I am not talking about who yells at them, but rather who notices if the kid needs a haircut and then takes him to get it.

Any working mother knows the difficulties of balancing a job and a family, but a woman in a traditional family business has an even more demanding and delicate balancing act because the business and the marriage become intricately tied together. To the extent that the woman feels a sense of power and autonomy in the business, then she can flourish therein. Oftentimes the amount of power is tied to the role the woman played in initiating the business.

Neither Rita nor Noreen initiated the business. Both chose to work in their family business as a transition while their children were young, their first priority being to stay home with them. As the children got older, they found less satisfaction in the arrangement. Neither of the women felt powerful or autonomous or that they could genuinely claim the business as their own. In fact, neither were legal owners. Although they could have tried to renegotiate the terms of their roles in the family businesses to have more power, they did not.

Both Rita and Noreen became convinced that if they wanted independence and creativity in their work, they would have to do so outside the family business, but extricating themselves was not easy.

Fortunately, not all women in family businesses feel this. For Gail Handeman and Wendy Repace, the family business proved ideal.

Gail Handeman

While Noreen and Rita were born in the mid-1940s and brought up to be traditional wives and mothers, Gail was born in 1956 and expected to pursue a career. She graduated from college in 1978 with a major in fine arts and moved to Chicago to get her master's degree in art history. She loved her work, as well as living in Chicago, but found that she couldn't support herself on an art historian's salary. At 25, she decided to find a more lucrative profession.

Opportunities for women in computer programming and systems analysis were opening up at the time, and Gail was hired as a trainee in the data processing department of a prestigious Chicago bank. Although never entirely intrigued with computers, she found the money attractive and liked the people she worked with. In fact, she met and married one of her co-workers, Phil Brunner. Like many women of her generation, she kept her name and her career after her marriage.

For the first five years, Gail was relatively content with her job. But as she approached her thirties, she became frustrated with corporate life. "It just got to be too much. I was working between ten and twelve hours a day, six days a week. And I'd get calls in the middle of the night if something happened to the system." In the back of her mind, Gail also began to question how she could have a child and continue this high-pressure, demanding career.

She watched her women friends struggle to take care of their babies and keep their jobs, and it was not a picture she found appealing. Her company offered no paid maternity leave and gave the impression that women with children were not considered as seriously as women without. Gail saw that basically the structure and demands of the business world are hostile to career people who want families. She knew that she had to make some hard choices regarding her career and children. Although Phil shared her concerns, he did not feel the same degree of emotional responsibility that Gail did.

At the same time Gail felt that before she made any major decisions about her future she needed some time for herself. To ensure that she didn't spend every evening in the office, she enrolled in a local cooking class. Not only did she discover that she enjoyed it immensely, she also saw how she might resolve her concerns about her future. As a favor, she helped her instructor develop computer software programs that recorded his recipes and inventoried his ingredient needs. This led to Gail's consulting for a few other local chefs on similar projects. She liked the challenge of using her computer skills for something she really enjoyed and found it quite a contrast to the bank job, which she had begun to detest.

Gail began to consider turning her cooking interests into a real business, thus freeing herself from the corporate world. Using contacts from her cooking instructor, she conducted a survey of chefs in major American cities to see if there was an industry-wide interest in her computer programs. She quickly discovered that there was not only extensive interest in such general programs, but also an interest in customized ones for special projects. She decided to start her own company.

Her ultimate plan was that Phil could eventually come into partnership with her. He shared not only her computer skills, but also her interest in cooking and her frustration with the corporate world. A family business would provide them with challenging careers and a life-style independent enough to let them create the type of family life they wanted.

Both Gail and Phil had had enough business experience to know they had to prepare both financially and psychologically for the strain that a new business can cause. Before Gail quit her job, they wrote a business plan that outlined benchmarks for the next three years. They decided that Phil would keep his job with the bank for at least eighteen months, giving Gail enough time to develop the computer software programs. She would earn virtually no money during that time. His income would shelter her efforts and also provide enough savings to pay for their health insurance once he had also quit. Until then, his company health plan would cover both of them.

Like most successful entrepreneurs, Gail and Phil were savvy and self-assured. They had confidence in their idea and in their ability to execute it. In fact, the only part of the enterprise that concerned them was the health insurance. For one thing, Gail had a hard time finding a company that offered maternity benefits on individual plans. Gail found this somewhat ironic: "This country encourages people to get out on their own and make it, but medical coverage for the self-employed is terrible. It costs way too much and sometimes does not even provide a full range of benefits."

Despite these problems with health care they decided to move ahead with the business. Gail quit her job at the bank and started to work at home on her personal computer, which she set up in the corner of their living room. She worked alone, often putting in sixteen-hour days writing and testing the computer programs. Phil sometimes worked with her in the evenings after he came home from his job. It was basically a solitary life for Gail and relatively austere for both of them as they were living on one income of $30,000 rather than two of that amount and were trying to save as much as they could.

As anticipated, at the end of the first year and a half she had the programs in line and Phil quit his job. When Phil entered the business full-time the dynamics of their life and home changed. They committed themselves entirely to the business, hiring two part-time employees and completely transforming their home into their office. Their personal lives and business became entirely inter-woven in their small, one-bedroom apartment. What had been a twelve-by-twelve-foot living room became Gail's office, in which she set up her computer, files, meeting area for clients, and work space for one of the employees. What had been their bedroom became Phil's office, in which he set up his computer, a work space for the second employee, and an overhead loft for them to sleep in.

They started working eighteen-hour days, six days a week, taking only Saturdays off. They no longer cooked at home because of lack of time, energy, and the sense that their apartment was a home. They relied heavily on take-out food and home deliveries. They were more likely to eat out of Chinese food containers than off their wedding china.

They never entertained because they had very little comfortable space, and when they did take time off they wanted to get out rather than stay in. They tried to keep the same sleeping schedules because Gail found it impossible to sleep in the loft if Phil was working away on the computer below.

Despite the strains of a new business and such close quarters, Gail and Phil discovered that they worked well together and could complement as well as duplicate each other's skills. Although Phil did some computer work, he assumed major responsibility for the marketing and sales of the programs, while Gail continued to control the programming. She insisted that he take the title of company president, as he would be working with the public, and she took the title of vice president. At first she was content with this division of work, but grew dissatisfied when she realized that clients never saw her and didn't take her seriously. "When they called the house they treated me like the secretary, and I didn't like it." She insisted that they switch roles in the business. Since their skills were so similar they had this option, which many couples would not have. Gail began to do the marketing and Phil the programming, although they kept the same titles.

Just as Gail felt that she was stereotyped because she worked at home, she also felt that their business was discriminated against for the same reason. To their surprise they discovered that certain credit card services would not extend charge privileges to their business, once they discovered it was based at home. This prevented them from taking credit orders over the phone or by mail—a serious impediment to sales.

Despite these problems, their family business appears to provide an ideal situation for Gail and Phil. They anticipate earning enough money to have children and move their entire operation to the country. They want a house with enough land so they can have a separate office building. This would provide maximum access between work and family areas but establish a clear boundary between the workplace and home. Two years in a cramped apartment has convinced them they need separate work and living spaces.

Just as they have learned that they can trade off roles in the business, they anticipate trading roles with their children. If one needs to work, the other will take care of the children. If the children are sick, they can both work late at night.

Their plan represents a practical realization of the abstract hopes of many young adults raised in the 1960s and 1970s—a desire to live closer to the land and achieve an independence in livelihood that is not easily accommodated by a corporate culture. Gail and Phil are of a generation taken with the notion of self-sufficiency. They came to maturity believing they had the power to change their own lives and the culture. Having experienced corporate jobs and the realities of cramped urban living, the prospects of using their skills for self-employment in pursuit of country living held appeal. In the abstract this is a fairly common plan, but not everyone has the resourcefulness and initiative to make it work.

For Gail and Phil having a family business at home appears to work. Although Wendy Repace and Tom Ritter have also been successful, they discovered that having a baby altered their expectations about the home as workplace.

Wendy Repace

In one of those odd quirks of life, Wendy Repace and Tom Ritter didn't meet until right after she had moved away from the city Tom lived in, Seattle. They spent the first four years of their relationship commuting between Seattle and Portland. In some ways it worked well, as both were recently divorced and reticent about marrying again. But in other ways, the situation grew intolerable and, in 1976, they decided to marry and to go into business together in Seattle.

Wendy had her master's degree in urban planning and had worked as a city planner for over ten years. Tom was a certified architect and had a well-estabished clientele in Seattle, but was ready to go out on his own. Theirs is an unusual family enterprise, because in effect they forged a partnership of two separate businesses. Wendy continued to work as a planning consultant, while Tom worked as an architect. Each works on his or her own individual projects, but occasionally they collaborate on one. Yet they think of their work as being one business, and they named the company accordingly—Repace and Ritter Associates.

Wendy and Tom are a study in contrasts. He is visual; she is verbal. He is low key; she is high energy. He is fair; she is quite dark. They complement each other and the dynamic works well in both their personal and business lives.

After their marriage, they bought a small, two-bedroom house in Seattle and converted the lower level, which is a walk-out basement with full windows, into a suite of offices. The larger room holds his drafting tables and desk; the smaller one, with expansive views of the city, holds her desk, books, and their computer. They bought the computer four years ago, a move which was crucial to their setting up a business at home. Having it meant they didn't need to hire a secretary, which was important because of the local zoning laws, which prohibited home-based businesses from hiring employees who were not family members.

Like many of the career women of the 1980s, Wendy put off the decision as to whether or not to have a baby as long as it was biologically feasible. But at age 39, she felt she should have one then or never. She and Tom spent a lot of time discussing how they could structure their lives in order to have a child. Both were career-oriented and ambitious and as a result both spent large portions of their time working. Although both wanted a child, neither wanted to give up his or her career to become the full-time caretaker. Nor did they automatically assume that Wendy would shoulder major responsibility for the baby. If they had one, they wanted to share equally in child care.

The fact that they had their offices at home is what finally convinced them they could handle a baby. They anticipated that having their work at home would solve all sorts of problems people face when both parents work outside. "We could trade off child care. One of us could work downstairs while the other would take care of the baby upstairs."

The realities of life rarely conform to expectations. Although Wendy had no difficulty in getting pregnant, she began to experience complications almost from the beginning, which forced her to change her work plans during the last four months of her pregnancy. Entirely bedridden, she had to cancel several projects that would have required her to travel, and she had little energy to write proposals for projects that would commence after the birth. When Benjamin was born Wendy was delighted to have a healthy, happy baby. But she and Tom discovered that it was not going to be easy to work at home and care for an infant. Before Ben was born they thought that they'd be able to coordinate their schedules so that one worked and the other cared for him or that they both worked while he slept or played. According to Wendy, "It hasn't quite worked like that. You can't just put Ben in a corner. When he is sleeping it is all right—for an hour or so, until he decides he doesn't want to sleep anymore. When he is up, he wants attention." Tom concurred:

> When he is in my charge, I can't get anything done. I have an L-shaped desk, and I can put him in his little seat on the side of the desk. I can set him there, hang a little mobile over the table, and he'll play with it for five, maybe ten minutes, and then he wants to sit in my lap. He'll sit in my lap for maybe fifteen minutes. I hang him over my shoulder, then he'll be comfortable for quite a while. But I can't get anything done, because I can't move my arm. So I really can't do very much when he is in the office.

Even when Wendy has Ben upstairs, Tom finds it hard to concentrate:

> My concentration goes way down when Ben is around. Even if Wendy is upstairs taking care of him, I am either wondering about it or feeling guilty that I am down here doing something, while she is upstairs dealing with him. Sometimes, I'll be working away on the computer, and Wendy is already upstairs getting dinner ready and Ben starts to kick up a fuss, so I usually just drop what I am doing and go up and take care of him.

The fact that a newborn infant is very demanding is not news to anyone who has children, but for Wendy and Tom it came as a surprise. Perhaps more surprising, in light of their discussions before the pregnancy, was that they found themselves reverting to a traditional division of responsibilities—but not without misgivings, at least on Wendy's part.

It has ended up that Tom is now the primary breadwinner and that bothers me. I realize that I just don't have the jobs because of my pregnancy and Ben's birth and that Tom does have the work. That's where our money's coming from now. I have to abide by that until I can do something. I realize that the only thing I can do now is to make some kind of day-care arrangements so that I have some solid time to write some proposals. Now I am just constantly picking up and putting down my work. It is just impossible.

The result is that Wendy spends time writing proposals for work which may generate money in the long run, but that currently brings nothing into the house. "My activities are just not as important. That is hard for me to take. I'm not used to it." Tom disagrees. "They are important. As far as bringing in money, no, they are not. But they are important. We made the conscious decision to have Ben, and we knew that we were going to have to take care of him for a long time. So this isn't such a big surprise."

Although sincerely concerned that Wendy feel her efforts are important, Tom's comments did not calm her—largely because he was indicating that her activities as mother to Ben were critical, while she feels bad that her wage-earning work is not now important.

Yeah, even though we sort of expected it, it's still unsettling when you are actually faced with the situation. When you're forty, and you're used to doing nothing but working, it's sort of hard getting used to taking care of a baby and not working.

Since Wendy has assumed primary child care responsibility, she is also physically separated from her husband and her own basement office. She now spends most of her days upstairs in the living quarters of their home rather than the office.

I just haul everything upstairs and keep it next to the dining room table. Whenever I have a chance, I sit at the table and work.

Sometimes I can do it, sometimes I can't. I put him in his little swing, until he decides he's bored and wants more than just swinging back and forth. Then I have to go pick him up.

Although her situation is less than ideal, Wendy thinks women who are completely alone are much worse off.

Even though I spend a lot of time taking care of him, it is nice to have someone in the house to talk to. We have lunch together. Ben gets to see his father during the day, which most children don't get to do. So far it has been a lot better than it is for most mothers and babies at this stage. Usually the father comes home, and he is tired and he never sees the baby except on weekends.

Wendy feels trapped, despite the advantages of her situation. She admits that she wants to have her cake and eat it too.

I knew that I didn't want to have a child and immediately go back to work and put him in day-care all of the time. As far as I can see, there's no point in having one if someone else is going to raise him. On the other hand, I knew I didn't want to stop working altogether. There's no way I'd be satisfied staying home. I'd go stark raving mad.

Wendy and Tom are at a critical juncture. For the first time in their eight years together their paths diverge rather than converge. Wendy has had to find a way to take care of Ben and pursue her career. Tom, on the other hand, has had to earn enough money to compensate for what Wendy is not bringing in. They definitely see both endeavors as partnerships, with each taking the lead in different areas. Wendy refers to Tom's work as "our" business and Tom refers to child care as "our" responsibility.

The need to earn more money means Tom has to expand. They have decided this can only be accomplished outside the home, since they need more living space and his architectural models demand more space than is available in their home office. As it is, models are everywhere: on the freezer, the washing machine, and any other available surface. Tom also needs more help, which means more room for additional staff. He could have contracted out the additional work, but this option did not appeal to him as he wants to have a full-service architectural firm. Because local zoning ordinances forbid nonfamily employees, the office has to move. According to Wendy, whose expertise is land-use law:

> Around here, you cannot legally have a nonfamily employee in a home occupation. We knew from the beginning that would eventually be a problem, but it turned out to be a problem earlier than we expected. The business is just growing so fast. The amount of business Tom has just expanded much faster than we thought.

The combination of the baby's needs and the expanded business forced them to decide to move their office out of their home and into an upscale commercial district. The implications of this decision concern Wendy.

> I am afraid that Tom's not going to leave the office until seven at night and I'll be home alone all day without anybody to talk to. I am going to be stranded there. Although I am going to try and get into the office as much as possible, I know I'll spend time at home, so I'll do some of my work there. It's going to be much harder now. I may end up having two desks for a while, one at home and one at the office. It's definitely going to increase my feelings of isolation.

Tom didn't foresee isolation as an inevitable consequence for Wendy. He felt that she shouldn't allow herself to get trapped, and insisted that they must bring the home into the office.

> I think that Wendy should bring Ben into the office and transfer our daytime home life there. She can come to the office any time of the day that she wants and she can go home any time of the

day she wants. The general rule is that she should spend much more time in the office than at home. And when she does spend time at home, it's because she wants to be there. In my way of thinking, we moved out *not* because of him, but because of space problems. We needed more space for the business as well as more space for the family.

Beginning to get enthusiastic, Wendy played off the suggestion.

What I might do is have the stroller there, and then I could take breaks and go out with the stroller and walk around the neighborhood. We have got the lake and park right across the street. In a way, maybe, if we could do that, it wouldn't be so different from the way it is now at home. It will be a little more intimidating because we will have to get our act together in the morning and get out of the house, but we can do it.

Wendy and Tom are pointed in two directions—tradition and change. On the one hand, they are reverting to more traditional roles and a traditional demarcation of work and family spaces. Wendy is the primary caretaker of Ben and is pulled toward the home; Tom is becoming the primary breadwinner and is pulled toward the outside office. Yet, they are unwilling to create polarized definitions of roles, places, and relationships between work and family. Even though they had to take their business out of their home, they do not want to take the family out of the business. They have few role models for accomplishing this but are determined to make their way.

Deirdre Cole

Deirdre's home-based business is now over fifteen years old. She started it as a way to supplement her husband's income, but it now supports her entire family. In fact, her success has allowed her husband Jesse to quit his job and work at home as well. Their story is about an evolving business and an evolving marriage.

Although neither were native New Yorkers, both Jesse and Deirdre were attracted to the city by the chance to work in the movie industry. Jesse moved there to take a job as an engineer in a sound studio, while Deirdre started out as an administrative assistant to a movie producer. They met through their work and were married in the late 1960s.

Shortly after the wedding, they found themselves unemployed; Jesse was laid off and Deirdre was stranded when her producer moved to Hollywood. With virtually no savings, they were forced to take a variety of odd jobs to survive. "We spent a year walking dogs in Central Park and living on hot dogs."

Then Esther, who lived in their Upper West Side apartment building and ran a market research firm out of her apartment, offered to take Deirdre on as an apprentice. The bulk of her business involved coding market research questionnaires that tested consumer responses to new products. She hired Deirdre as a coding assistant. Jesse does not have fond memories of those times. "I was doing some free-lance sound recording work for motion pictures, but it was definitely not stable. It was scary for me, which is why I went back to a regular job with a stable paycheck with a studio as soon as I could get one."

By that time Deirdre was pregnant. Since she definitely wanted to be home to raise her child, she decided to stay with the market research coding job, even though she had initially seen it as just a tide-me-over until Jesse got work and she could find a better job outside the home.

After Sean was born, Deirdre worked four to five hours a day in Esther's apartment taking Sean with her. When Sean was two, Esther decided to retire and offered her clients to Deirdre. It was too convenient to turn down, so Deirdre moved the coding business into their apartment. At that time, it was a one-person show that neither Deirdre nor Jesse took too seriously. Jesse saw himself as the traditional breadwinner. "I felt responsible for the entire family. For a long time, I just thought she was playing around and wasn't really working." At that time Deirdre shared his view.

At the beginning, it seemed reasonable for Jesse not to take me seriously. Our marriage started off with him being the breadwinner and I just assumed that my work was not that important. I had that little administrative assistant job when we first got married, and Jesse had his job, which was more important.

But as Deirdre got to like her work, the less she felt that way about it. After four or five years, it had become obvious to both of them that her work was really a major part of her life. But as it grew in importance, size, and complexity, it caused some problems for him and made their home life fairly complicated.

Deirdre and Jesse live in a medium-sized, two-bedroom apartment. The living and dining area form an L with a galley kitchen. Although a good-sized apartment by New York standards, it was barely adequate for the combined needs of a family of three and a business that employed up to seven people at a time during rush periods. In addition, Deirdre encouraged her employees who had infants to bring them to work. "Having a baby around just keeps everything in perspective for us. When things get hectic or tough, you can cuddle or walk the baby and things just kind of fall into place."

For the first fourteen years Jesse worked outside the home. He and Sean would leave at 8:30 for work and school respectively and Deirdre's workday would begin shortly thereafter. It was typical for her to have five employees arrive for work around 9:00. The workday was supposed to end at 5:00, but during busy periods, and when a deadline loomed, her employees and their children were often there long after. "Jesse used to hate coming home and finding people working here."

He disliked the disruption to his living room and felt his life was being invaded by his wife's employees. "I used to come home and reach for my cider and it was all gone. I would scream 'Who's been drinking my cider?'" Jesse started to leave signs on his food and Deirdre tried to keep separate shelves in the cabinets and the refrigerator for family food and business food, but the boundaries were frequently violated. The border warfare over food was symptomatic of the difficulty Deirdre had at first in separating her work from her family.

For the first several years, Deirdre used their joint checking account and their home telephone for her business. This also drove Jesse crazy. "I used to go bananas when checks were written to these kids out of my checkbook. And then I'd get my phone bill that was ninety-five bucks. I'd say, 'Who the hell's making all these phone calls?' Finally, I just said, 'Get your own checking account and your own phone.'"

Doing those two things was the turning point in Deirdre's professional evolution, for the first time she began to think of herself as a business owner. This was further solidified when she got her business cards and stationery.

Despite these changes in her self-image she continued to manage the business as if it were an extended family. She'd cook lunch for her staff everyday—at one point they all went on a diet together and she'd cook special meals. She took care to hire workers who were able to maintain a certain ambiguity about their roles. They were often called upon to serve as baby-sitters. If Deirdre was tied up with a client, one of her employees would play with Sean, take him to the park or out for ice cream. Sometimes Sean would help out. In fact, Deirdre maintains that he learned to write his name because he had to sign for so many United Parcel Service packages. The ticklish times were right when he came home.

Invariably our busiest work times are between 3:30 and 5:30 every day, just the time Sean got home from school. I would always try to stop and give him a hug and then go back to work. If he really needed me, I'd stop and talk. He sometimes had a hard time understanding that I was here but that I was not here for him. He did not understand that I work.

Over ten years, as Sean got older, Deirdre was able to devote herself more and more to the business.

> I have much more energy than I had when I was twenty-five. Sean is fifteen now and he doesn't need the same amount of attention he needed when he was little. There was just so much to do. Childbearing and child rearing took so much time. I'm beginning to believe in the biological clock—that women don't come into their real essence until after they've raised their children. I find that I don't care how other people think about me. I am much more mellow and I feel comfortable with myself and what I am doing.

At 40, Deirdre felt she was "just getting to the good stuff." Her husband, on the other hand, had begun to question some of the beliefs that had guided his life. In contrast to Deirdre, he felt his energy waning. "I think as you get older the internal fires work less and their energy gets less. I have nowhere near the energy now that I had when I was twenty-five. I am a little tired."

In recent years, Jessie's career as an audio engineer had been put in jeopardy by technological advances. Rather than being upset about being phased out of the industry, he has seen it as an opportunity to reflect on his life.

> I look at people riding around in limousines and eating in expensive restaurants and I think, how come I didn't get to that point? But the other side of me says, "I couldn't stand to continue the push that they have to continue to stay there." I want to be able to enjoy my life. I have begun to question the values that I was taught as a kid. About a year ago I got to the point where I was really dissatisfied. I started to question what it was that I was *supposed* to do, as opposed to what it was that I *wanted* to do. They were in conflict with one another.

Jesse began to question the values that his father had taught him about what it meant to be a man.

My father taught me that you have got to make it on your own, that you are responsible for the entire family, and you have to prepare for their future. My father was a very successful man— much more successful than I am. He kind of instilled in me the belief that I had to do it all. But I look back and say, If he was so successful, why was he so unhappy? Why did he put so much energy into providing for the future and he never enjoyed the now?

In his mid-forties, Jesse decided to figure out what would make him happy. For more than ten years, he had enjoyed playing with computers. He decided to turn that avocation into a business. At 45, he quit his job at the audio studio to take some time off and develop his own computer-based consulting business. Until his business develops enough, he has agreed to help Deirdre in hers.

Deirdre and Jesse are obviously at very different stages in their individual lives. Deirdre has never had more energy. For the first time in her life, she feels that she can devote her full energy to her work and is only beginning to hit her stride. Jesse, on the other hand, is ready to slow down and reflect. For the first time in his life, he feels that he has the luxury to question. Just as child rearing precluded Deirdre from pursuing her work fully, it also precluded Jesse from examining the meaning of work in his life.

The success of Deirdre's business released Jesse from his financial responsibility as breadwinner. The year that she made enough to pay all of their monthly expenses was a turning point in their relationship. They had choices they had not had before, and decided to switch roles.

For the past two years, Deirdre has been the breadwinner and Jesse's been more of the homebody. For most of the first year and a half Jesse was not motivated to give his all to his business. He wanted the luxury of taking time off altogether from work. That was hard for Deirdre to accept. "I don't mind supporting the family, because I believe that Jesse will become a financial support for the family. But I just wouldn't want to be married to someone who didn't want to play, too."

Neither Jesse nor Deirdre feel that they could have undertaken this type of role reversal during the early stages of their marriage. Jesse said, "We didn't understand each other enough, and we weren't forgiving of each other enough." Deirdre added, "We imposed all of our own perfectionism on the other. We believed that if I can do this, you can do it, too, if you really love me." As a result, everything became a test of love. Over time, they have accepted that they are simply different.

They have also recognized that they have very different ways of dealing with stress and anger.

> Jesse yells all the time. He's a banger and a yeller. I am sarcastic and a sulker. We're lucky that after all these years, we understand there are different ways to get angry. I am sure Jesse hates my sarcasm and sulking, as much as I hate his banging and yelling, but that's just the way things are. Neither of us is going to change.

This level of understanding allows them greater possibility for working together, but they haven't eliminated all problems. Right after Jesse quit his job, Deirdre hired him to do what she refers to as "mindless sex kitten work" such as ripping apart pieces of paper or sorting questionnaires. With all her other employees, Deirdre would tell them exactly what to do:

> I have my own little paper-by-the-dozen efficiency theory. I will tell you what hand to hold the paper in and how to rip it. At first I tried to tell Jesse, but he would get crabby. All my other workers would have told me, "I hate it, I don't want to do it. Give me something else." But Jesse wouldn't. He felt obligated. But it was clear that he didn't want to do it and he just wouldn't say so.

Yet, he'd always question her on how she did things, and it drove her crazy. She was used to running the business and setting the procedures and not being challenged on them. Eventually she stopped hiring him for those types of tasks, but occasionally he would then work as her part-time secretary. Even that posed some problems because Deirdre would treat him differently from her other employees. "I hate to admit it, but it's because he stays here and the others go home."

It is clear that they are not in a partnership. It is her business and he occasionally works for her. Each wants it that way. She has run her business for too long to suddenly begin thinking of it as "their business." He wants to start his own business anyway. While he is getting started he is willing to work for her, but he definitely sees that as temporary work and as helping her out.

In some ways her business is becoming his client. When she gets a contract that requires computer analysis, she subcontracts the work to Jesse. They have been conscientious in trying to clearly define their professional territories, and those boundaries are reflected in their apartment. Each has staked out a portion of their apartment as his or her own territory, and each reigns supreme in that territory.

The living and dining area are Deirdre's business area. As Jesse says, "When I go in there Deirdre is the boss." The master bedroom, where the computer is, is Jesse's territory, and he is the boss. As Jesse says, "The physical doorway between the living room and the bedroom marks the boundary, and everybody seems to honor it." But since these rooms are also the family home, unusual circumstances can arise. For example, one day Ruth, one of Deirdre's employees, had to do some computer work. She went into Jesse's "office" to work. Jesse recounts the episode:

> Ruth was in there working, and I went into the bathroom, which is right off the bedroom. I never shut the door since it is our bedroom. So this time I didn't shut the door either. So, I'm in there talking to Ruth and all of a sudden, I say, Oh, my God, I'm standing here with the door open talking to Ruth.

Deirdre also has problems with the fact that his office is their bedroom. Their jobs are intense and Jesse can't do the computer work until she finishes the coding, which means that sometimes he can't get started until late at night. She has to prepare the data and get them into the computer, and then at night he starts to manipulate them. But Deirdre has difficulty in stopping. "I have a problem when he is working on one of my jobs. I feel like I have to lie on the bed, fully dressed. I don't feel like I can go to bed when he is working on one of my jobs."

If she had a choice, Deirdre would never again let their bedroom be used for an office.

If we move, we are going to have a very small bedroom and it's going to be a boudoir. There will be no computers, no file cabinets, no work. If your office is there, where is the intimacy of the bedroom? Now, I know why the lights are always off when we go to bed. I mean, who wants to look at the computers? She longs for more separation between her work and family.

Sometimes, I look up in the middle of the day and want it to be my house. I want everyone to just go away. Sometimes I feel totally invaded. And it's particularly rough if my son or husband are home sick. They want to stay home and be taken care of and I have got work to do.

Not all family businesses are alike. In each case, the family business mirrors and expresses the basic marriage relationship—whether the terms have been openly negotiated or are unspoken and implicit.

How a man and a woman define their roles in a family business depends in large measure on how they define their roles in their marriage. If they live as breadwinner and helpmate, they likely will extend those roles into the business. The man will initiate the business; the woman will assist. He will assume the most public role; she will be behind the scenes. He will most likely own the business, although they will speak of it as theirs. He will draw a salary, while she will be unpaid. How satisfied the women are with these terms depends to a large extent on how satisfied they are with the terms of their marriage.

If a couple suspends the definitions of roles found in a traditional marriage, they can find a resiliency in a family business that does not exist in the world of conventional work. Since there are no rules for running family businesses, the man and woman have the freedom to sit down and negotiate how they want to divide responsibilities. They must decide who will assume responsibility for all the aspects of the business and of the family. As with Deirdre and Jesse, a family business can provide the framework for radically restructuring the roles in the marriage. As Wendy discovered, it can also provide the shelter for one partner to take time off and raise a child but maintain a sense of professional identity.

5

Empty Nesters

All of the women we have heard from thus far were born in the 1940s or 1950s and started to work at home while they had young children. They tell only part of the story about women and home-based work. There is another generation of women, born in the 1920s and 1930s, whose stories are different. These are women who started home-based businesses later in life—after their children were grown and gone.

Many women find it difficult to enter or reenter the work force when they are in their forties and fifties. Many jobs seem trivial or demeaning after decades of responsibility and being in charge of one's self and family. In the past the tremendous energy and enthusiasm of women at this stage in their lives might have been devoted to volunteer work. Now they want to direct it to wage-earning work, and often harbor a dream of what they'd like to accomplish. A home-based business offers some an attractive way to achieve such dreams.

This chapter tells the stories of three women who fought hard to live their dreams. Like the other women we've seen, their decisions about work were intricately tied to circumstances in their marriages.

Janet Tillman

Born and raised in Southern California, Janet Tillman dreamed of a life as a fashion designer, but an early marriage cut short those dreams. In 1952, at the age of 19, she wed her high school sweetheart. They moved to Fresno, California, where he worked as a production supervisor at a small manufacturing firm. She worked as a secretary until 1954, when she became pregnant with their first child.

"I come from the old school. We women didn't have hard choices. Family always came first with me and I didn't have to find an alternative to being a full-time wife and mother. I was very content to be home." She and her family could live the 1950s American dream—a house in the suburbs and two cars—on one income. Middle-class mothers of young children were expected to be at home rather than outside holding down a job. In fact, more than two out of three mothers stayed at home in the 1950s—quite a contrast from the 1980s, when nearly two out of three mothers work.

Throughout the 1950s and 1960s, Janet led an active and demanding life as the mother of three, feeling powerful and respected in her roles as full-time wife, mother, and homemaker. "I was in command—I was responsible for my entire family and had to make sure that everything ran smoothly." She did all of the cooking and cleaning, was active in her children's schools, and was perennially a den mother or Brownie leader. Her volunteer work on behalf of her children provided her opportunities to use and develop her natural organizational and leadership skills. It was a life-style that suited her personality and their family circumstances.

As her youngest son reached adolescence in the early 1970s, Janet faced the fact that her responsibilities as a mother would shortly end. "I knew I had to start preparing for the day when I would no longer be a full-time housewife and mother. I am a high-energy, take-charge person, and I knew that I had to find something to do after they all left home."

Rather than expanding her work as a volunteer, Janet decided to get a paying job but insisted that it be only part-time. "I couldn't work eight hours a day with all my responsibilities at home. My energy would not have spread that far." To her surprise, this take-charge, confident woman found that the marketplace was not ready to greet her. "Employers would say to me, 'You haven't worked in nearly twenty years, so you don't know anything about office procedure.' But I knew a lot more than I was given credit for."

Her frustration grew to indignation that employers didn't value the skills required to manage a home and family successfully. "Job applications should have recognized those skills. If employers ever did an inventory of all of the skills used by housewives and mothers, they'd see an incredible number of demanding skills. Instead, they wanted 'marketable skills' and they said that I didn't have them."

Eventually Janet was hired as a part-time file clerk in a local accountant's office. It was better at least than working as a sales clerk or waitress, but her new job was far from satisfying. "I found myself in a job where I worked for a man young enough to be my son and that wasn't easy to take. I had all this experience and knowledge and I had to work for someone who knew less than I knew." In her home she was a respected, powerful person, but in the office she was a powerless subordinate. This contrast in status was hard for her to take, but she decided to tolerate it as long as she had children at home who required most of her energies.

As her youngest son approached his senior year in high school, Janet decided her time had come. "One day I sat down and said, 'Hey, what do I really want to do?' For the first time I had the privilege of doing what I wanted to do and the chance to be happy in my work. I didn't care what I made so long as I loved the work."

Her attitude toward a job mystified her husband, Gordon. Raised in the Depression and taught to be the breadwinner, he could not understand placing a higher premium on work enjoyment than on money; his responsibilities had taught him otherwise. For years he had supported a family of five, including some very tough times.

Janet believes that their different attitudes toward work are based on their different family responsibilities. "Gordon has to support the family so he equates a job with money—making a certain amount of money in a certain amount of time. But I don't. Whatever I make is great, because I don't have the pressure of earning $1,200 a month to pay the bills. If my earnings go up or down, it doesn't matter because I don't have to support the family. He does."

Although they have had disagreements about her earnings, Gordon and Janet have an openness in their marriage that allows them to air their differences, rather than letting them fester beneath the surface. Although Gordon will never entirely understand her views, he no longer feels he has to. In his mind, Janet has fulfilled her important responsibilities—to raise three healthy happy children—and is entitled to do something for herself. For Janet that has meant creating a work situation that mirrored her experiences as a homemaker.

She wanted independence to control how and when she worked, and she wanted creativity—both of which she'd enjoyed as a full-time wife and homemaker. Her future as an employee looked bleak; she had little interest in working for the next twenty years as a file clerk. Self-employment held more opportunity for her than did outside employment.

Janet was not alone in her assessment. Many older women take real estate licenses, work on commission for large sales companies such as Mary Kay or Tupperware, or start their own businesses rather than take the kind of office or retail jobs typically available to them. Some women draw on their domestic skills and start service business, such as catering, sewing, or cleaning. Others draw on skills they developed before they had children.

A crack typist before she got married, Janet decided to build a secretarial business. "I figured if I could organize someone else's office and do all the typing, why couldn't I do it for myself?"

Basing her business at home offered her some advantages. Since she would have virtually no overhead and limited requirements for capital investments, other than a typewriter, the home provided the most financially sensible location. But there may have been an additional symbolic reason for starting the business there:

her power was in her home. Janet had felt powerless in the business world beyond her front door, and she was much more comfortable establishing her business in her home than outside it.

Janet calmly set out to lay the groundwork for her business, drawing on the organizational and leadership skills she had developed as a homemaker and volunteer. She spent hours in the local library doing research on typing businesses, then turned her attention to her community, surveying local businesses to determine the potential market for her services. She priced her services by calling typists listed in the yellow pages of the telephone book and pretending that she was a potential client who wanted estimates for particular projects.

Having done her basic market research, Janet then attended a one-day Small Business Administration (SBA) seminar that provided information about bookkeeping, record keeping, and taxes for small businesses. The seminar provided the final boost to her efforts. She knew it was time to claim her space at home.

Unlike women who set up their typewriters in the kitchen, Janet was definitive about the need for a separate office, cut off from the traffic of the home. "I came home from the SBA seminar and my youngest son was in his room packing for college. He had boxes all over. I walked in and said, 'Well this is my office.' He said, 'What? Give me a break, I'm not gone yet!' I said, 'You're gone, this is my office.' I could just envision it."

The room suited her needs perfectly. It was on the first floor off the living room, with separate doors leading into either the kitchen or the foyer. Its large windows afforded an expansive view of their tree-shaded side yard. It offered the privacy and the light that she wanted, and Janet felt no ambivalence or conflict about usurping it for herself. Her son would always be welcomed at home, but just as he was ready to start a new phase in his life, so was she.

Establishing the office was the first tangible symbol that she was a business owner. Within days, she ordered business cards and printed flyers, confirming the fact. She wasted no energy in distributing her flyers to local businesses. "I took the flyers around and said, 'I am starting a home-based secretarial typing service. If you have overflow work, call me instead of a temporary agency.' The local merchants took me in like a child and said, 'I'll be glad to refer work to you.' I began to get walk-in clients from these businesses and students from the local university."

As the business got going, she enjoyed the money she was earning but disliked the lack of control she had over the pacing of her work. After two months of undependable piecework, she decided to find a way to get steady contract work. "I started to think about where I could go to get consistent work. It dawned on me that court reporters need transcribers, so I got out the telephone book and under the yellow pages, it says, 'Reporting, Court.' So I started calling agencies. An agency five blocks away said, 'Yes, we need a transcriber.' I didn't know anything about transcribing but I can spell, so I took the work."

Janet's organization, self-confidence, and ability to push on and adapt were rooted in the fact that she had felt strengthened by her roles as wife and mother and not undermined by them. The respect and dignity she felt in those roles carried over to her expectations and abilities in her work. When she was dissatisfied she reevaluated her needs and developed alternative solutions. If the solutions required risks, she thought nothing of taking them.

The fact that Janet and Gordon can talk about their problems has enabled them to respond to their changing needs at different stages in their lives. Gordon is nearing retirement and wants to take off long weekends for fishing. Janet wants to make a success of her business, which often requires her to spend over forty hours a week working. But the fact that she owns her own business and runs it at home gives her the ability to meet her needs and yet be responsive to Gordon's. She will often work four very long days, so she can take off three days with him. They'll pack up their camper on Thursday night and take off. She was able to take a month off so they could take an extended camping trip through Alaska, an unlikely possibility had she continued to work as a file clerk for someone else. Although their relationship balances well there have been times that Gordon has had to revert to drastic action to keep Janet from becoming carried away by her work.

When I first started my business I spent so many hours on it that I think he felt left out, especially on the weekends. One Saturday, I was sitting in my office with the doors shut. I had my headphone on and was transcribing. I was really concentrating. Pretty soon one door opens up. I look up, and he goes out through the other door and closes it. I think, I wonder why he did that? So I started typing again. Pretty soon the door opens again; he goes through and he closes it. It begins to dawn on me that something is different each time he goes through, but it hasn't yet clicked. The next time the door opens—and he is stark naked. That did it.

Karen Wilkes

Karen was born in Galesburg, Illinois, in 1936. The youngest of three daughters, she was raised on a farm. Since they had no brothers the girls helped out with every aspect of the work. "We did a little bit of everything—harvesting, butchering a cow, driving a tractor, and keeping the books. We had to learn how to take care of ourselves."

At the same time, Karen was expected to conform to the patterns and habits her older sisters had established. "By the time you're the third daughter, things are old. Everybody had done everything by the time it got to me. I got so tired of following two sisters through high school. There wasn't much freedom. We all did the same things. We wore bobby sox, took piano lessons, belonged to the YWCA, and sang in the church choir."

And they were all expected to go away to college, preferably to girls' schools. Her parents placed a high value on attending college, due in large measure to the fact that Karen's mother had gone to college in the 1920s and expected her daughters to have the same opportunities.

Both Karen's sisters went east to girls' colleges. Like two of their aunts, they each decided to major in education and it was assumed Karen would do the same. But she would have none of it.

She had no interest in teaching school and absolutely no interest in going to a girls' college, no matter how good it was.

She enrolled in the University of Illinois in 1954, choosing home economics as her major. At first glance, that seemed like a very traditional female occupation, as well as a respectable substitute for teaching. But Karen had other intentions for her home economics training. "Something kept pushing me toward home economics—food was a big part of our lives. My mother was a great cook, and we had loads of parties. We all learned to cook from the Betty Crocker cookbook, which was real popular in those days. All through the cookbook were photographs of 1940 kitchens and ladies in uniforms. Those pictures captured my imagination."

Not only did those pictures capture her imagination, they also showed her how she could get into business. Those women in the cookbook were the first business women she had seen, and they became her role models.

When she graduated from the University of Illinois in 1957, she used her home economics degree to get a job in the test kitchens of Procter and Gamble in Cincinnati. She worked there for two years, grateful to be working with one of the top marketers of food products but bored by her job. She also saw limited oportunities to advance out of the technical work she was doing. "My supervisor encouraged me to leave because she said, 'It's a man's company,' and she was right so I quit."

At 24, Karen found herself free to explore her options and decided just to enjoy interviewing for jobs around the country. "There were a fair number of jobs at the time and not that many qualified people. I flew to Philadelphia and was offered a job with the *Farm Journal*, which would have been nice. I went to Chicago and was offered a research job. But then someone told me about a job at a Columbus newspaper, so I thought, 'Well, I'll just go up there and see what it's about.' I knew nothing about newspapers, nobody in my family had ever been in newspapers, but they offered me the job."

Karen was hired as the food editor for the daily paper. "It was the most fantastic experience. I learned all about food photography, I got to cover all sorts of events, and I learned to write under deadlines. I was having a ball." And she was thoroughly enjoying the reactions of the old-timers on the paper. "They would say 'Who's that young girl doing the food? Can she do it?' But I proved I could do it, I won their respect, and I learned a lot. I felt like I had been let out of a cage and could fly."

Despite her love for the job, Karen was not immune to the social expectations of the late 1950s. "Even though I was working and loving it, in those days women didn't have career paths or objectives. We were raised to be wives and mothers—that was supposed to be our big ambition. If you didn't get married a year or two out of college you were odd."

As she approached her twenty-sixth birthday, Karen's family and friends began to pressure her to "settle down." Although they thought that what she was doing was interesting, they saw it as a diversion until she got on with what should be her main direction in life—which was to be a wife and mother.

Karen started dating a fellow reporter who worked on the city desk. He was talented, bright, and funny, and within a year they were married. Although she wanted to continue to work, she quit when she got pregnant with their first child. "I never considered keeping my job because I was thinking 'MOTHERHOOD.' At that time women didn't do that. Once you became a mother, you just didn't go off and leave your kids."

But she never really made a conscious choice in the matter or seriously deliberated other options. Staying home was what a woman did. Her husband earned enough, so she didn't need to work, and she couldn't justify working for any other reasons. Working for enjoyment would have been considered selfish, and might be considered abandoning her children.

The first several years were very hectic. Karen's family moved from Columbus to Chicago. When her first son was three, she had her second, and then her husband decided he wanted to move to France for a couple of years and write. Always ready for an adventure, Karen thought it a great idea. They lived in Paris while her husband worked on a book. Before he finished it they ran out of savings and returned to the U.S., where he took a job as a junior editor for a publishing house in New York. They rented a small, three-bedroom house in the suburbs and Karen became pregnant with their third child. The book never got finished. The following year, 1969, Karen gave birth to their daughter.

They lived a very conventional suburban life. Karen's husband would commute into New York City by train every morning, leaving her at home with three children under the age of five. Unlike some wives, Karen found she was not well-suited to being a housewife. "I was home all day. I had three little kids. I didn't know anybody in the neighborhood. I never got the house stuff done and I felt trapped. I would never buy the newspaper even though I loved to read it, because I thought maybe if I didn't read the newspaper, I'd get the curtains up or get the house cleaned. It was a bad situation—it was the pits. I didn't know what I was going to do."

Karen lived like this for several years, never understanding what was happening to her. Here she had been a successful newspaper woman who took risks and loved a challenge, and now she found herself as a housewife who could never finish anything and whose self-confidence had vanished.

She was as baffled by her husband as she was by herself. He couldn't keep a job—by that time he had been let go from the publishing job and voluntarily quit his next one as a reporter at a magazine—and he wasn't ambitious. "In my family, the mother raised the family and the father earned the living. I expected my husband to do the same. But he didn't. He was so talented but could never keep a job. I never understood why he couldn't get ahead, why he wasn't ambitious."

Karen did not understand why she was still interested in a job; why she was so unhappy staying home as a mother; why her husband showed no drive or initiative in his work. None of this fit her image of what marriage should be. She should have been content to stay home and he should have been out slaying dragons for his family.

"My relationship with my husband began to deteriorate. There were problems between us that we didn't address. We could never talk and we never resolved our problems. It was frustrating because here we were two awfully bright, smart people, but we just seemed to sweep everything under the rug and act like nothing was going on."

Their situation got worse rather than better. "My husband started a new job working for a small publishing house in New York City, but the bottom fell out of the book business. He was a junior person and lost his job. He couldn't deal with that. Along came this young woman who just thought he was the cat's meow. And this guy went. He just copped out entirely. There I was—renting the house, three little kids, and no money."

Within months her husband moved in with his girlfriend in New York City, while Karen stayed in the suburbs with the children, totally unsure as to what she was going to do next, or even where she was going to live, and still unable to talk about how she felt. "My mother came out to stay with me, but I was too proud to admit even to her how scared I was. She was supportive, but I was just too proud to discuss any of this with anyone."

Finally Karen decided, more out of pride than anything else, that she'd stay in the East. "I was determined not to go back home to Illinois—no matter what—so I started looking for a job." At first, she wanted a job in the immediate area and was willing to take virtually anything so that she could be near her children. "I had the 'guilty-mother syndrome'—I've got to be near my family, I can't leave my kids." She feared that if she went to work in New York City her children would feel abandoned by both parents. But she got over that guilt pretty quickly, when she discovered the kinds of jobs available to her in the immediate area.

I was offered a job in a candy test kitchen, but I decided that I couldn't develop and test recipes with chocolate every day. I thought, oh, my God, I just can't do that. I decided I would rather type letters all day than work with chocolate. And I really didn't want test-kitchen work. I had done that kind of work when

I first got out of college and I didn't want to go back to it. Gradually, I got up my nerve and thought, maybe I can work in the city.

New York City represented the big time and she was terrified of it. Although at 24, Karen had felt courageous and capable of taking risks, at 37 she felt unsure and lacking in confidence. Marriage and motherhood had eroded rather than strengthened her confidence —a reaction very different from the one that Janet experienced. Although close in age, Janet and Karen were far apart in attitude. Janet's self-esteem had flourished those years at home, while Karen's had faltered.

Financial circumstances forced her into action and she called some old contacts from Columbus to help her get a job in the food industry. "One of them put me in touch with a public relations firm right in midtown New York. This PR firm hired me on the spot because I had been a food editor for a major newspaper. I took it. They paid me $10,000 a year, and I got my foot in the door. It was a good time—1973—before a lot of women went back to work and I was a little older than the ones right out of college."

Although the firm valued her skills, Karen was scared that she might not make it and was determined not to cause trouble for herself. "I didn't say 'Boo,' when I first started there. I didn't have any self-confidence and I had so much to learn." She listened, she learned, and she worked very, very hard. She had become the sole provider for herself and her three children and she could not risk losing that job.

Meanwhile, her husband had become the nurturer. Without speaking they had switched roles. "Once I started commuting, my ex-husband and his girlfriend moved back out here. He'd come over in the morning and feed our kids breakfast; he'd get them off to school; and he'd take them to the doctor and dentist. He'd come here after school and feed them their evening meal. He did everything I thought I had to do."

By being the helpmate, he allowed her to be the breadwinner. "It was perfect, because I could never have done the PR job if I hadn't had his support. I sometimes would not get home until nine or ten at night. And by the time I got home, I knew that the kids would have had their dinner, done their homework, and taken their baths. He really supported me through all this and was a very good father."

They discovered that they were both better suited to their reversed roles than they had ever been to the conventional ones assigned them. "I discovered I was the ambitious determined one. I loved working; I loved commuting. I just wasn't cut out to stay home. I was a very excitable and impatient person, but he was very calm. He was the better parent."

He was very patient with their children and also very good on discipline. "He always used to say to me, 'You be the adult.' I kind of learned from him how to deal with the children." Although he never had much money, since he supported himself just on his free-lance writing, he was entirely generous with his children. "If he had anything, he'd share it with the kids. He traveled all over Mexico with them; he took them for snorkeling courses; he made sure they were certified divers; he taught them car repair and carpentry. He spent a lot of time with them."

Karen realized that her husband's role model for a father was very different from hers and that his actions made complete sense in light of those influences. "I figured it all out. He comes from a family where the mother is dominant. His father is a nice gentleman, but a real Casper Milquetoast. The father got his two boys off to school and really did a lot of things around the house." In other words, his father was not the breadwinner, nor was he dominant or ambitious. His mother embodied all those characteristics. Without realizing it he had married a similar woman. Yet it took their divorce before they found the roles that suited their personalities.

During the time that Karen was working out her home life, she was also engaged in a complicated relationship at work. When she was initially hired, she was assigned to work as an assistant to a woman with a home economics degree and twenty years experience in public relations. Karen came to view Lois as her mentor, and Lois embraced the role. Early on Karen realized that they worked together well because of the way their needs meshed.

"I was this meek little soul. I just wanted to do the work and earn the money. That was great for Lois because she wanted to be the star. I would do all the work, and she would get the glory. All in all, she was a little insecure, but I got along fine with her because I was a good backup and I didn't want to be in charge."

Karen worked as Lois's assistant for over eight years, at which time Lois decided to start her own agency and asked Karen to join her. "I was glad to get out of there. I didn't like the quality of the work they had begun to turn out." Karen had begun to develop her own standards and had found the firm too limiting. She quickly discovered that Lois's firm was equally constraining.

The situation deteriorated as Karen continued to mature into a confident and independent professional. "I knew Lois's thinking on everything. We began to get in each other's way." Some mentor relationships can absorb that type of maturation and some cannot. Karen discovered that hers could not, but she was intensely ambivalent about initiating the split. "I had been with her ten years and I knew we just couldn't stay together forever, but I was so scared. I couldn't give up my salary, because I had still had these kids. I kept trying to be the good employee, but I had my own ideas and I knew I could stand on my own now. I didn't need her to fight my battles anymore."

Before Karen could decide what to do, Lois fired her. "It was really brutal. She called me in on a Friday afternoon and said, 'You're fired. Clear out your things today.'" Lois tried giving reasons, but Karen rebutted every one. "I was pretty strong by that point and I think she was amazed. I didn't cry or throw tantrums or anything. My son came to meet me a few minutes later and we packed up my things and I said, 'Nothing like going home with a mother who's been fired.'"

She walked out the door carrying two bags of her things and never went back. She walked into her home an hour later relieved that she no longer had to play the good employee, and terrified about how she was going to support her family. One son was already in college, the other was starting in September, and her daughter was in a private high school in Manhattan.

"I decided that I wanted to start my own food public relations business." She had three months' severance pay plus unemployment insurance to cover her, and she threw herself into the business, putting out the word to former clients and colleagues that she was starting her own firm promoting new food products through newspaper articles and television coverage. She began to design layouts for food advertisers. Within a month she had two small retainers, plus a few short-term contracts. It was tough at first, "We sort of lived hand to mouth for a while." But she was willing to go into debt in order to ensure that she made a success of her business.

Although her years with the public relations firm provided most of the professional skills she needed, her farm background gave her her financial savvy. "Growing up on the farm taught me that you have to spend money to make money. We had to borrow money to buy cattle, so we could make money." She's convinced that these early experiences on the farm rid her of the fear of money that many women have. "I learned to be willing to borrow and to think long-range."

Her financial responsibilities were great the first several years, but her home responsibilities were minimized by having her sons away at school, which gave her the time and space to establish the business. She converted what had been the boys' bedroom into her office, setting file cabinets against the wall, and a drafting table and desk under the window.

Having her daughter at home put some boundaries on her business, because she would quit in the evenings to fix dinner and talk with her. Had she not been forced to break off work during that first year, she might have burned out. "It would have been easy to just keep working out of my fear and anxiety that the business might not make it."

Karen now lives alone and takes great pleasure in how her life has turned out.

It took me a long time to get here. I am fifty-one years old, I now have got what I want and I like it. It was worth working for. I don't have any regrets. I take time for personal things. People like my work and I see my business growing. I have a nice standard of living. I don't want to live rich and spend a lot of money. I just would like to make enough so I can live comfortably and do some traveling and give some money to the arts. My most immediate objective is to get my kids educated and that's happening, so I see a light at the end of the tunnel. It is exciting that they are getting the education they want. They have all gone to the schools they wanted to go to, and they are very individualistic, independent, hard-working kids—that makes me very happy.

Unexpected events, like her divorce and firing, forced Karen to take control of her life. But not all women wait for such circumstances to jar them into action. In her forties, Pat Briggs decided it was time to examine the terms under which she had lived her life, forged her marriage, and defined her work.

Pat Briggs

"I always did what I was supposed to do. I graduated from college. I got married. I married the man I was supposed to marry. I had my children when I was supposed to. I always did what my mother expected me to do. I never disgraced her."

Pat Briggs excelled at being the dutiful daughter and all that it entailed. A stunner in high school, she was elected senior prom queen, went to college to get her teaching degree so that she would always have something to fall back on, married right after her June graduation in 1956, never having taught, and within three years gave birth to Robert and Janice.

During the next fifteen years, Pat was a devoted wife and mother, an attentive daughter, and a successful manager of a law office, having picked up paralegal training along the way. As she approached her fortieth birthday in the fall of 1974, she began to suffer chronic pain from ulcers, pulled back muscles, and migraine headaches. She had always had the headaches, but the combination of ulcers and back pain nearly incapacitated her.

Pat was certain that her problems were related to stress. She broke with her social upbringing enough to go into psychological counseling because she began to think that her discontent was related to being the dutiful daughter. "I realized that I couldn't deal with all of my mother's expectations for me."

She also realized that her mother's expectations were symptomatic of the broader social climate in which her mother had grown up and in which Pat had been raised.

When I think back to the 1950s, we really got caught up in a whole bunch of things that never really gave us time to sit back and think about ourselves. Gals were brought up to believe that you went to college, became a teacher or a nurse, got married a year or two out of college, and then had your kids. Today a lot of gals take the time to be themselves before they get married—if they get married. We couldn't do that in our twenties. If we had done something like that, our mothers would have been carting mountains on their backs to atone for us. I was doing what my mother expected of me because that was what her mother had expected of her.

Through her therapy and discussions with friends of similar ages, Pat grew convinced that the social climate of the times, including her mother's expectations, precluded a woman from making real choices in her life. The lack of choice and the sense that she had no freedom in her life were taking a real toll on her health. "I finally realized that I was not doing what I wanted to do and I certainly was not doing what was good for me."

So at forty, Pat Briggs decided to take the time to explore what it would mean to be herself. "I decided that the time to be myself and to grow as a person would come toward the end of my life, rather than at the beginning or the middle. But I was determined it was going to be there and that I would get the most out of it."

Once she began questioning the lack of choice she had exercised in her early life, she became sensitive to the types of choices friends made in their later lives. Her next-door neighbor's experiences proved to be a catalyst to Pat's thinking. Although a few years older than Pat, Barbara was brought up with the same expectations. She graduated from nursing school in 1952, got married, had her kids, and worked part-time as a surgical nurse until the early 1970s, by which time she was tired. She was tired of nursing and of constantly going to school to keep up with all the new developments. When her kids were in high school she decided to try something different and enrolled in a painting class, where she discovered a talent she had never known she had.

She began painting murals on the outside walls of buildings. Her sense of color, texture, and scale created a demand for her skills, and within several years she was traveling around the country painting modern, expansive wall murals. She loved what she was doing and had never felt so happy and challenged. Her husband was in full support of her work as were her children, by then in college, who were delighted to watch their mother blossom. Her experiences had only been positive and she encouraged Pat to give some thought to what she might really enjoy doing.

Although Pat enjoyed the intellectual challenge of her legal work, she felt it lacked any real creative edge, and she was intrigued by Barbara's experiences. "I thought it would be really great if I could make my living sewing." She had sewn since she was five years old. She was not only very fast—able to turn out a dress and sometimes two a week for family and friends—she also had a good eye for fabrics and design. She always designed her own clothes using a pattern only for basic proportions. Barbara's experiences inspired her to toy with the idea of selling her work.

Once she was open to the possibility, she was graced with serendipity. While in the Caribbean for vacation, the manager of a small boutique in which she was shopping asked to buy the coat dress she was wearing. When she realized that Pat not only had sewn it but had also designed it, she offered to buy as many as Pat could produce. That experience gave Pat the first taste of making money from doing something she loved. But, like Janet, she was slow and cautious. She decided to start sewing enough to sell at craft fairs, then see what the response would be before making any deeper commitment to a custom sewing business.

She kept her job at the law office, working thirty hours a week, but spent an increasing number of hours at home sewing, often putting in fifty hours or more a week. She loved the satisfaction of working on something that stirred her soul. "I probably have some repressed urge to create, and sewing is creative. I can get up at four in the morning if I want to do something that just suddenly comes to my mind. I am not restricted. I have no boundaries. I am not filling some niche that someone else has set for me. I am doing what I want to do at my own pace in my own time."

In the process, however, Pat began to spend less and less time on household matters such as cooking and cleaning. She began to do some traveling to craft shows. When her husband came home at night there was not always a hot meal waiting for him; in fact, sometimes there was a note telling him what was in the freezer. If he made social plans for them that conflicted with her work schedule she'd speak up, insisting he go but that she had to stay home. If he was upset, she wasn't as likely to make the effort to cajole him into a good mood as she had before. In order to keep her job and pursue her sewing, Pat had changed in ways that did not please her husband. He was not ready to shift in his expectations for their marriage.

Throughout my entire marriage, I had subordinated to him. By starting something on my own, by having to travel to market my work, and by being successful, I changed. I was no longer what he had in mind for a wife. I was no longer able to come home after work and wait on him. I was becoming very different than the wife he had known for twenty years. I was more outspoken, more independent, and less submissive.

Although she liked those changes in herself, her husband did not. Barbara's husband had encouraged and supported her evolution, but Pat's husband was threatened, and their marriage broke up. Pat received no child support or alimony since her children were already in their early twenties and she had worked for years in the law office. This change in her financial situation forced her to give serious thought as to how she would survive, particularly looking ahead to her old age.

"I became more calculating about sewing as a business, because I have no pension plan at the office. In my particular administrative category there are no fringe benefits." Like so many women, this situation never bothered Pat when she was married, because she was covered by her husband's health plan and would have access to his pension funds later in life. She had never anticipated getting a divorce and having to take fringe benefits into account.

> But after my divorce, I suddenly looked at myself and I thought, Where am I going to be when I reach 65 and there is nothing but this virtually dormant Social Security system? That's when I decided to build my sewing into a big business. I felt that it was something I could build on as long as I started then and gave it enough time to grow.

Pat knew that she would have to be patient about the time it would take to develop her sewing into a full-fledged business, anticipating that for the next six years she would keep her job at the law firm and build the sewing business on the side. She needed the law job for its stable income and the sewing and design for its creativity.

Although she works long hours and bears the financial responsibility for her daughter's college education and all of her own monthly expenses, she has an energy that is generated by living life on her own terms. Unlike her early years, where she fit her life into the niches created by her mother's and husband's expectations, Pat now carves out the contours according to her creative needs.

Although any divorce is difficult, Pat maintains a friendly relationship with her husband, feeling that they unfortunately just outgrew each other. Interestingly enough, she has grown into deeper and more satisfying relationships with her son and daughter. The stronger she has become in her own right the stronger her relationships with her children have become. "My children tell me that I am an entirely different person, that I am more confident and that I amaze them with what I am doing and want to do. I love it. Until now I always felt that there was such a huge gap between us—I was the mother and I was stuck in this little hole. Now I realize that it was because I wasn't happy with myself. Now I am. I have my own interests. I am creating something on my own."

Despite the fact that she loves what she now does, she is not convinced that as a young mother she could have undertaken the kind of commitment that her sewing business requires. "As a mother you are very much aware of your responsibility for your children. When you have the responsibility for someone else, whether a child or an aging parent, you can't really take any risks, because if you take a risk and you fail that risk and failure will affect them. And you can't do that; you have too many people depending on you."

Part of Pat's belief about the constraints of motherhood may also be tied to the fears that she herself experienced as a mother of young children. She was the type of person who had great difficulty in relating to small children. "I would have been marvelous with my children if they would have been born as adults. I was so nervous. I was so afraid that I was going to do the wrong thing. I was so afraid that I was going to put them in some life-threatening situation or do something awful so that they'd turn into idiots by the time they were thirty-five. I never had the time to enjoy them."

As she grew confident in herself, as her children got older, and as she assumed total financial responsibility for herself, Pat began to see ways to create wider vistas in her life.

Unlike most women in home-based business, who either work alone or hire one or two employees, Pat has dreams for creating a large-scale business that would hire home sewers nationwide. In the summer of 1986, the Secretary of the U.S. Department of Labor proposed that the forty-four-year-old ban on home sewing of women's apparel be repealed. This federal action could open the way for Pat to execute her dream.

> I want to start a business that would employ retired and handicapped people. It would provide them with income. The retired people could do it without being tied down into a schedule or being pushed into a higher tax bracket or forced to give up their Social Security benefits. It would be super to hire handicapped people in their homes. They are marvelous workers; if they take a job, they finish it. Some of them are slow, but that doesn't make a lot of difference, because others are fast—so it would even out.

Pat wants to create a business based on win-win principles. "I think if you do something for people that builds up their morale and their pride in themselves, then you have not only helped them but you have made yourself feel awfully good. I am convinced that this business is going to make other people happy and that it's going to give me enough to live on."

Pat no longer has ulcers, headaches, or backaches. If she is tired, it is because she works long hours. But she loves the life she has created for herself and calls her home, where she does her sewing, the "Yankee Clipper"—a fast-sailing American ship. It is moving forward and she is the clipper's captain. "I never dreamed that I would live life on my terms and be doing something creative. But I am much happier."

Women who gave birth to their children in the 1950s are as different from one another as women who give birth in the 1980s. Some, like Janet, wanted to stay home and were happy and at peace with the decision. Others, like Karen and Pat, were not content.

Where the 1950s clearly differ from the 1980s is in the prevailing expectations for women. In the 1950s, women were expected to stay home. Janet wanted to, and probably a large measure of her peace was due to the congruence between her individual choice and the broader social climate. Karen and Pat deviated. Both tried to fit themselves into the times, but both suffered. Karen became depressed, disorganized, and unable even to complete the daily routines of living. Pat, on the other hand, incurred a range of physical ailments. Yet neither saw a way out until they got older. Only then, as they began to respond to their life situations on their own terms rather than by responding to conventional expectations did they begin to experience satisfaction in their lives.

Janet ruefully discovered that employers were not interested in her skills as a homemaker, not recognizing their applicability. Janet is one of millions of older women in our society who took time off to raise children only to discover limited opportunities for interesting and challenging work later on, amid an abundance of jobs that pay little and challenge less. Fast-food restaurants, shopping malls, and offices are filled with talented older women who take jobs far below their skill levels. Sometimes they do it because that is all they can find or want, but other times it's because their confidence has been eroded by the mixed messages given them as mothers. Rhetoric places high value on motherhood, but employers penalize women for having taken time off to raise their children.

Janet's self-esteem was strong and capable of overcoming the resistance of such attitudes, but not all women are so lucky. Some women internalize that negative message and end up afraid to try for a job that might really interest them. Having spent years fighting for others, they often have lost the confidence to fight for themselves. The unselfishness thought necessary to be a good mother does not always serve a woman well in a competitive job market. Indeed, some employers take advantage of this psychological vulnerability. One office manager on Long Island said, "I specifically looked for an older woman who hadn't worked in years because I knew she'd work hard and wouldn't speak up because she'd be terrified of being fired."

Karen knew that terror when she took her first job on Madison Avenue after her husband left her. She was lucky, since she at least got back in the game after ten years away, and she worked hard to keep the job. But there were limits to her advancement opportunities, largely due to the alliance she had forged with her mentor.

Pat never knew terror in her work, but she did know it in her life, when she felt it slipping away as she lived it on other people's terms. As she became aware of what interested her, she saw no way to pursue it except through self-employment. In pursuit of that goal, she now holds two jobs and works over eighty hours a week.

All three of these women turned to a home-based business as the best way to achieve the independence, creativity, and power that was unattainable for them in the conventional world of work. All had worked too hard in their lives, raising their children, to sell themselves short in later years. For the first time in their adult lives they find they have the energy to devote to a work effort that pleases them, and they want the satisfaction of that experience.

These three women are survivors and probably will always be happiest working on their own. But for other women, who would like careers in more conventional workplaces and professions, it would be good to examine how the business world's structure of advancement and success is tailored to the lives of men—particularly men who do not have child care responsibilities. What the stories of these three women indicate, perhaps more powerfully than anything else, is that there could be another way to chart a career, which would take into account the periods of child rearing and utilize the skills and energy of those who raise our children. Unlike men, who typically are ready to slow down in their work as they reach their fifties, these women are ready to hit their stride.

6

The Negotiators

In this chapter we are introduced to the most clear-cut success stories of home-based work. We have already seen that some women are better equipped and able to work at home than others. These stories clarify how some women have successfully negotiated the conditions necessary to success.

First, there is the matter of personality. These women see themselves as independent; they do not feel tied to the notions of how they were brought up and what other people expect them to be. They define their lives on their own terms.

Second is the matter of conviction. They all hold strong notions as to what they will and will not accept at work and at home, and are at peace with the decision to work at home. When the situation ceases to please them, they negotiate alternatives.

Third is the fact that they don't assume that other people know what they want. They figure out what they want and explicitly negotiate the conditions under which home work will give it to them. If married, they establish the rules of the game with their husbands—defining where they will work, the hours they will work, and what their husbands can or cannot expect of them while they are home. Unlike women home workers who feel bombarded by the house, the errands, the delivery men, or the plumbers, these women do not allow those types of intrusions into their work time or their workplace.

They go deaf when the house starts making demands to be cleaned or attended to or if other distractions threaten. If their work involves clients, they set the conditions: when the clients call, when they can come to their home, and what they can expect. These women set boundaries with their husbands, their children, and their clients—boundaries that are explicit and enforceable.

Beth Stover

Starting a home-based word-processing business was not a long-term dream for Beth Stover. Getting her doctorate in political science and being a writer was. After graduation from college in 1976, Beth immediately started her graduate studies in political science, at the University of Wisconsin. She had long entertained notions of being her generation's Simone de Beauvoir, living a contemplative life as a writer and thinker.

With that goal in mind, she completed a master's degree and began course work for her doctorate, but in 1980 decided to spend a year in graduate school studying philosophy at Columbia University.

While she was finishing her master's in New York City she met Richard, a freelance composer who lived in the city. Within months, Beth was married and pregnant and having to decide what to do regarding her doctorate. This was not a turn of events she had anticipated.

If she wanted to complete her degree at UW-Madison she had to return for another year of residency, write the proposal for her dissertation, and then pass her comprehensive examinations (which involved five days of written tests and one day of oral defense) to qualify to write her doctoral dissertation. This would mean spending at least two more years in Madison, and possibly longer if she was going to stay there while writing her dissertation.

Now that she was married and soon to be a mother, she did not want to return to Wisconsin alone, yet she didn't see a way that she and Richard could go together. Richard had no interest in leaving New York, nor was Beth convinced that the college environment would suit his personality or professional needs. She also had become ambivalent about investing more of her life in graduate school, given the limited availability of university openings for assistant professors. In addition, New York City had begun to work its magic on her and she found herself enjoying its dynamics and atmosphere.

After several months of deliberation, Beth decided to forgo the doctorate and stay in Manhattan. Two months later she gave birth to Aaron, a long, lanky blond eight-pounder, and found that she quickly needed to get a job to supplement Richard's income. Although she had no business experience, her analytic training and writing skills actually provided her with considerable leverage in the information worlds of finance, publishing, and writing.

When Aaron was three months old, Beth was offered a research and writing job with a New York management consulting firm. Given the fact that she had an infant son and that Richard was traveling a fair amount on writing assignments, she set the terms under which she'd accept the job. "I took the job on the condition that I'd leave at five o'clock sharp, because I had to pick up my son at his sitter's."

For the next four months, she'd arrive promptly at 8:30 each morning and leave at 5:00. Then one day her boss decided that he needed to start meeting with her at 5:00 every day. Beth was surprised, but said it was impossible given her family commitment. Her unwillingness to change her schedule displeased him, and their working relationship began to deteriorate.

By that time Richard had landed what appeared to be a stable position writing music for commercials, giving Beth the opportunity to quit her job and take some time to decide what direction to pursue next. But her reprieve was short-lived. A change in clients cast Richard's job in jeopardy. "We had $500 in our savings account and we spent $3,000 a month, so immediately I had to get another job."

The thought of going out and walking the streets job-hunting turned her stomach. The short time that she had worked as an employee in the business world had convinced her that she was not suited to working for someone else.

Beth disliked having little control over the amount or pacing of her work. "I hated not being given enough to do, but being expected to sit at my desk and look busy. It was such a waste of my time." She resented being supervised by someone whom she considered to be her intellectual inferior, and who treated her poorly if he was in an off mood. "If he had a bad day, he could step on me and get away with it." Furthermore, while office politics intrigued others, they sickened her. "I hated getting caught up in petty gossip and that sort of thing. It was a waste of my time."

Unlike many people who love the culture of a workplace, with its political dynamics, unspoken rules, rituals for advancement, and various forms of feedback from paychecks to promotions, Beth was entirely uninterested. "I am a loner. I am very private. I enjoy my time by myself, and I really don't like to knuckle under to someone else. It always has been a problem with me."

Whether she had a problem subordinating or simply had a high need for independence, one thing was absolutely clear—she wanted a work environment that was entirely under her control. If she had to earn money she wanted to do it on her terms. Yet she more or less fell into the business she eventually started.

"We had a personal computer and two printers at home and I said, 'This is crazy. Why don't I start a business at home?'" She decided to start a word-processing business as a way to earn enough money to cover their expenses and give her the control and autonomy she wanted. The same desire for control that made her unhappy as an employee facilitated her efforts to set up a successful business at home. She converted the dining room of their two-bedroom apartment into her office and immediately recognized that she needed advice and information on running a business. By calling word processors listed in the yellow pages Beth located and joined a guild of typists and word processors that had been started by a typist several years earlier.

She was quite clear about the clientele she wanted. "I wanted to enjoy the work I do; I wanted it to be educational and exciting, so I decided to focus on developing professional and creative clients." Drawing on her husband's extensive network of friends and colleagues, Beth quickly developed a client base of psychiatrists, writers, playwrights, professors, and lawyers. She charged them $20 an hour, $5 less per hour than what other members of her guild charged, which did not please them. They pressured her to raise her rates, but she resisted. "The problem is that most of the people I work with are self-employed like me and they really can't afford higher rates. It's been a trade-off for me. I have wanted to do interesting work, so I have been willing to keep my rates lower to keep these people as my clients."

Despite their disagreements over her rates, the guild has provided an indispensable support group for Beth. They meet once a month to discuss various aspects of business ownership, ranging from how to do their taxes, to how to handle difficult clients, and how to respond to recent advances in computer technology for word processing. In addition, they provide backup help to any member who has overflow work, gets sick, or wants to take a vacation. Explicit rules about how to handle someone else's clients have been accepted to ensure that no one member "raids" another. The guild has remained a relatively select group because the members want to ensure that they maintain comparable high standards of quality in their work and in their professionalism in dealing with clients.

The guild has provided Beth with the type of information and contacts that very few home typists have access to. Not only do members keep each other abreast of business information, they are also constant emotional supports. One of the major problems for many home typists has to do with self-esteem. They often, like Beth, back into typing or word processing at home with only a vaguely defined sense of themselves as business owners or professionals. The guild stressed both components of these roles and by becoming a member Beth quickly came to see herself in those terms, getting away from the tendency not to take her work seriously. The guild also provided an antidote to the loneliness of working at home, making one a member of a community of small independent business owners within the larger community of business owners. New York City is large enough so that there is sufficient work to keep many word processors busy, so competitiveness among the various guild members is not a factor.

There has been much discussion about the exploitation of home workers. The guild provides an important example of how they can organize to protect themselves. Members of the guild charge prevailing market rates and provide advice and assistance on how to deal with clients whose expectations are unreasonable or who do not make payments.

Beth was sufficiently well-protected to earn a healthy income of $40,000 her first year as a word processor. She typically worked forty hours a week, although occasionally worked more if under a pressing deadline.

For both professional and personal reasons, Beth established a conventional work schedule; nine to five, Monday through Friday. Unlike many home workers with preschool-aged children, Beth did not try to work around the sleeping and eating schedule of her son, nor did she work when he was in the home. "At his age, he is very needy. It would break my train of concentration if I had to pay attention to him and try to charge someone an hourly rate. Neither Aaron nor the client would get treated fairly." She or Richard took Aaron to his baby-sitter's home every morning at nine, and one of them picked him up at five, freeing both parents to do their work during the day.

Beth was determined to treat her home office just as she would an office outside the home. Just as she would not have taken Aaron to her office when she worked at the consulting firm, she would not take him to her office at home. Therefore she needed child care just as she would have with an outside job. Although working at home did not eliminate Beth's need for child care, it did provide her with more flexibility. If there was an emergency Richard or Beth could be there immediately, because the baby-sitter was right around the corner from their home. And in case of illness, she had the ability to switch her hours. Beth preferred taking Aaron to a baby-sitter rather than having one come to their home. Having him at home would have been hard on both mother and child. She felt he wouldn't be able to understand why he was being kept from her, and she didn't want to face the guilt of hearing him cry but having to stay at her desk.

Despite the prevalent notion that one can run a business at home while taking care of children "with your left hand," our national survey showed that one out of every two professional and clerical women working at home rely on some help with child care. The professional women were more apt to pay for help; the clerical women more often relied on unpaid help from family members. If they had no help, they often did their work late into the night. Rarely did women actually work and care for their children simultaneously, particularly if their type of work required any concentration.

Beth's desire to keep strict business hours—something she would not have been able to do if she worked around Aaron's sleep schedule—also reflected her intent to maintain a professional image for her business. Other home-business owners have confirmed the fact that clients take them more seriously when they take themselves seriously, and one way of expressing that seriousness is keeping regular hours. Just as you expect your doctor or dentist to have an office and set hours, so do the clients of home businesses. There's an interesting psychology at work that transforms some of the flexibilities of home-based work into drawbacks. If a business owner charges low rates, is available to meet at any time, and will accept clients dropping in at all hours they will be taken less seriously than someone who charges prevailing rates and is firm about when they are and are not available. In addition to keeping strict hours, Beth put a second phone line into their apartment and only answered it during work hours. Although her clients came to respect her work schedule and its boundaries, her husband was much slower to do so.

When they moved into their pre-World War II apartment building on the upper east side of Manhattan, Richard converted the maid's room into his office where he composed every day and some evenings. When Beth started her business, she took over the dining room. Every morning they would go to work in their respective offices. All would be fine until he would hit a snag. Then he would want to take a break, and she was there. He would interrupt her whenever he wanted to, regardless of where she was with her work. He'd suggest that they go to the museum, take a walk, make love, or simply sit and talk. Beth is crazy about her husband and enjoys his company, so this was very distracting for her. After several months of this pattern of constant interruption, she insisted that he get an office outside the home. Richard was not keen about her suggestion, and he dragged his feet, although intellectually he knew she was right. Exasperated, Beth went out one day, looked over a couple of possibilities, and signed a lease for him. He now works several blocks from home in a small studio apartment. Now, during the day, Beth works alone at home. Aaron is at his babysitter's, and Richard works in his office. Beth has control of the work space she needs.

She is still having difficulty with the fact that her husband doesn't see eye-to-eye with her about housework. Unlike many women who feel compelled to assume more of the housework responsibility since they're at home during the day, Beth feels that housework should be divided.

My husband is a very sweet man, but very devious—although not consciously so. He wants a nontraditional wife but a traditional home, which means he wants me to work, but he also wants me to take care of the house. He tries to get out of doing any work in the house, by saying, "Look, work is work. If I have

more time to compose, I will make more money and pretty soon
we will be raking in the money. The sooner that happens the
better."

Richard believes that since he earns more per hour than Beth
and has a greater earning potential overall, he should be released
from having to do any of the shopping, cleaning, and cooking. That
way he can spend more time getting rich. He argues that the division of household responsibilities depends on earning power and
that the person who earns less should be the one to do the cooking, cleaning, and shopping so the person who earns more is free
to earn as much as possible. She completely disagrees with him—
for several reasons.

You don't measure a person's worth by how much money they
make. Furthermore, it is a matter of choice. I don't choose to do
housework. I hate housework. I hate doing the laundry. I hate
shopping and I don't like cooking. I don't like doing those things
any better than anyone else does. But they are things that have
to be done. I don't want them dumped in my lap just because it
gives him more freedom to go off and be rich and famous. I want
a choice as to whether or not I do those things.

Beth has perfectly enunciated one of the most common unspoken assumptions of marriage: the more money a partner makes
the more power they should have to do what they want. The corollary to this is that the less money a partner makes the more they
should do what the other doesn't want to do.

Beth undermines this assumption by her belief that one does not
work only to get rich. She works at word processing because she
likes doing the work. She could earn more doing something else,
but she would lose too much that she values, so she is willing to
trade off some of her earning potential for the opportunity to have
autonomy and exercise creativity in her work. And she is unwilling
to subordinate her job to Richard's simply because she earns less
than he does. Beth will not let money define the division of power

and leverage in their marriage. As a result, she will not entertain his notion that she should do more housework than him. Beth is rare in that she has confronted this question and rejected the standard assumptions.

Even the most professionally savvy women frequently accept an unfair division of housework because they earn less than their husbands. In effect, they feel that they are somehow required to buy themselves out of these responsibilities. If they earn more, then they can demand more of their husbands in terms of housework and errands. Unfortunately, they may find themselves in a Catch-22 situation—never able to devote enough time to earning more because of the responsibilities they assume for housework and child care. It is difficult in this context ever to earn enough to "buy" equality with their partner. By accepting the assumption that money and power in a relationship are linked in this way, they allow the rules of the marketplace to define the dynamics of their intimate relationship. Beth has refused to accept this.

Richard is not too happy about it, but I am sorry. I just have to feel that I am being treated equally and fairly. If I loved doing housework or if I got some fulfillment from doing it, then it would be a different story. But to me it is slave labor. I love my son and I spend a lot of time with him, but I don't get a big kick out of doing his laundry. I don't like standing in line at the grocery store any more than anyone else does.

She insisted that the household chores should be divided on an equal basis—and each of them would assume complete emotional responsibility for making sure their half got done.

I said to my husband, "Pick any five chores. Pick the five easiest, I don't care, but just pick five. I'll do the other five. I don't want to remind you, I don't want to nag you. I am not your mother, I am your wife. So just do them." He may not enjoy them, but I mean who really enjoys them? My attitude is if he chooses the laundry, he is responsible for the laundry. If he doesn't like doing it, then he can take it out and have it done or he can hire someone to come in and do it. I don't care how it gets done, just so it gets done. If he chooses shopping, I don't care if he does it at five in the morning or ten at night. The grocery is open twenty-four hours a day.

The vast majority of women would be grateful if their husbands "helped out more." Beth doesn't want to be "helped out," she wants equal division of responsibility, and refuses to be responsible for delegating and directing her husband around the house.

When Beth forced Richard to confront the situation he was clearly not thrilled with the idea, but he did go along with her. Once they divided up the tasks, he was on his own. "He has to know that if he doesn't do it, then it won't get done." If he didn't wash the clothes, they weren't washed. She was not going to step in and save him.

Her firmness about this clear division of responsibility is part of the discipline by which she keeps the house itself from distracting her from her work and its demands. "Just because I am here doesn't mean that I should be doing those things. Women are accustomed to doing all those things themselves. We tend to take on all these responsibilities and it's just not necessary."

Beth's success in establishing the conditions under which she can work at home is largely based on her and Richard's relationship. Richard wanted a nontraditional wife and a traditional home. Beth is for the nontraditional wife, but she insisted that they have a nontraditional home. Their partnership has been resilient enough to accommodate this arrangement, particularly her rejection of the unspoken assumption that money buys power.

Linda Cook

Although she is the same age as Beth, Linda Cook's family situation is entirely different. She and her husband, Terry, have no children, and from the outset they have divided the housework and shopping equally. Linda's main task was to negotiate a work schedule that accommodated Terry's schedule.

She and Terry moved to northern California from Minnesota in the early 1980s because Terry wanted to finish his degree in engineering at the University of California at Berkeley. At that point Linda was ready to break with the expectations that her father had for her, which had heavily influenced her life up to that time.

Linda was born in Minneapolis in 1951, the younger of two daughters. Her mother was a full-time wife and homemaker and her father a successful entrepreneur who owned a furniture factory. She and her sister were raised in a traditionally conventional manner. "We were brought up to be a nurse, a social worker or a teacher. You would never have considered a male profession. My sister became the good speech therapist and I became the good teacher."

In 1973, Linda completed a degree in special education at the University of Minnesota, tried teaching for several years, and then quit. She didn't like the combination of low pay, high stress, and limited respect, and began to consider going into her father's business. By the mid-1970s it was becoming more accepted that a father could bring his daughters, not just his sons, into a family business. Unlike the family businesses discussed in Chapter 3, which were small and service-oriented, her father's business was a major factory. In 1977, Linda went to work for her father.

"He didn't give me any breaks or advantages just because I was his daughter. He said that if I wanted to work for him, I would start at the bottom and work my way up, which was fine with me. I learned how to run a business from the bottom up. I did everything, from bookkeeping to marketing to sales."

She discovered that she enjoyed business much more than teaching. But after several years, she also realized that she did not want to stay in her father's business for good. She and Terry, whom Linda had married in the late 1970s, decided to move to California. "My father was very disappointed when we decided to leave Minneapolis. When we were at the airport, he even said to me, 'You are the last person who can take over the business,' and I said, 'Well, that's fine, but that's not what I want to do.'"

Linda was certain it would not have worked. Her father would always treat her as his little girl, and as long as he lived would not have been able to relinquish control. "He had a lot of difficulty in separating an adult-adult relationship from our father-child relationship, and he never completely treated me like an adult. I didn't want to get further involved in the business."

Shortly after they arrived in the Bay area, Terry started at UC Berkeley, as planned, and Linda supported the two of them by doing bookkeeping for a local firm. After Terry graduated, she decided she was too smart to stay with straight bookkeeping. "So, I went back to school, took all the credits I needed for an accounting degree, and sat for the Certified Public Accountant [CPA] exam."

In the back of her mind, Linda had already decided that she wanted to start her own company, but to be certified she first had to work under supervision at an accredited accounting firm and be approved by them. Linda landed a junior position with a large accounting firm and worked her way into tax accounting. She hated the experience of working for someone else.

"The entire time I was at Allendale Weiss, I felt like I was on hold. It was like a jail sentence. I was paying my dues and didn't really enjoy it. I felt so stifled. The only thing that kept me going was knowing that one day I would get out of there and do what I wanted."

Like Beth, Linda had discovered through trial—and, in her opinion, error—that she was unsuited to working in a big organization. Part of her frustration was that she felt she could earn much more out on her own.

She was the ultimate pragmatist, however, and made the most of her apprenticeship. "Unbeknownst to them, they allowed me to learn a lot about running a business, by putting me in charge of lots of different projects. I was also able to meet people, to make contacts, and to develop certain technical skills." The firm sheltered what proved to be the first stages of Linda's own entrepreneurship. They also provided her with the idea for her own business and her first set of clients. As they were very pleased with her work, when she quit two years later they subcontracted a great deal of work to her, providing, in effect, a solid base of clients.

When I worked there, I was in charge of a department that recruited small businesses as clients. After a while the company figured that small clients were not cost-effective for them. So when I started my own business they contracted this small-client business out to me. I would do the bookkeeping for these small clients, then I'd send them back to Allendale Weiss at tax time and they would do their tax returns.

Everyone benefited from this arrangement. The client was satisfied because Linda charged them less than the big firm would have. Allendale Weiss was satisfied because they only had to prepare the returns, without having to do the bookkeeping cleanup. Linda was satisfied because she got out of the company and out on her own with a fleet of clients. She estimates that 90 percent of her clientele comes from Allendale Weiss.

Linda decided to locate her business at home entirely for financial reasons. "I would be silly to go out and rent space and cut into my profit. My overhead is so low at home, my tax deductions are so good, that I end up with a high profit."

Although it is financially sensible to work out of her home, she was concerned about its professional implications. She discourages clients from coming to her home for fear of appearing less than professional. Linda and Terry live in a small, two-bedroom attached patio home in a new suburban development in Orinda, California. Although their living room windows and deck offer expansive views of the surrounding hills, Linda's office is set up in the lower level in the second bedroom of their home, so that clients must walk through the entire living space to get there.

If we had a larger home where there was a separate entrance to my office I would probably let more clients come here. But since my office is in a spare bedroom I don't. I think I'd lose some of my credibility and my professionalism if I let people traipse through my house to get to my office. I like to maintain a professional edge, so I go to their offices.

Some women back into starting a business of their own. For Linda it was a deliberate and positive move. "I am a one-woman show and I get a lot of ego satisfaction and gratification from being in business by myself. I am in control and I am completely running the show. It is a power trip."

Given her ultimate ambitions, she does not want to be completely seduced by the power trip.

It's okay for now to do it all myself since it is my first year in business, but to be honest, I want to get to a point where I can kick back and let all the drones do everything for me. I don't know if this is what I want to do the rest of my life. If it helps me accumulate a nest egg that I can parlay into another entrepreneurial business that'd be great, but I don't envision that ten years from now I will be this little drone bookkeeper, typing out all my own statements.

She already feels that it is time to delegate some of her responsibilities. She would prefer to have someone else type the statements, answer the phone, and run errands. "I mean, that stuff is beneath my skill level. I am ready to hire someone to help, but economically I think, 'Why should I pay someone to do it when I can do it myself and not have to pay?'"

Linda's business is at a critical growth stage. If she hires someone it will dramatically cut into her profit margin, but if she doesn't she may not be able to grow at the rate she would like because of the workload.

In the interim, and as a transition until she decides what to do, Linda has come to rely heavily on her husband. He supports her emotionally, he provided the financial stability she needed to quit her job and start the business, and he pitches in to help when there are serious deadlines. He once spent an entire week sorting through a client's "records," which consisted of two shoeboxes full of receipts. Linda attributes her courage and support to him. "I don't know if I would have been so bold and ambitious to go out on my own without him. He has always been supportive. When I first discussed the idea of a business, he said, 'Well if you think you can make a go of it, go for it.'"

Despite his support, Linda had a difficult time establishing a schedule for herself. Trying to work at home reminded her of her experiences as a college freshman. "I had been so restricted in high school that when I went to college, I just went crazy. I didn't know when to study or when to sleep or when to play. When I first started the business, it was kind of like that. I'd sleep until nine, and then I wouldn't get dressed for a couple of hours. I'd fumble around and then maybe start working about noon." By the time Terry got home at six, she was deep in her work and ready to keep at it until nine or ten. "Finally I thought, This is really screwed up. We are on two entirely different schedules and I never get to see Terry."

Terry wasn't too happy with the arrangement either. He couldn't figure out why she was working at night when she had the whole day to work—why couldn't she start at eight in the morning so they could have the evening together? Terry's dissatisfaction was a major factor in getting Linda onto a structured nine-to-five schedule, which she prefers.

Maintaining that schedule gives her a clear sense of the beginning and end of her workday. "Now if I want to do an exercise class, I'll do it after work." She doesn't want to slip back into her earlier unscheduled situation, which allowed her to procrastinate. She also finds that the daytime schedule works out better for her clients: they know when they can reach her and she can keep limits on her accessibility. She had to control the telephone to make this work. Since Linda doesn't have to commute, she can sleep until 8:30 and still be at her office at nine. "I have had clients call me at eight in the morning and wake me up. They'll ask if they woke me up and I'll say, 'Well, yes you did,' and they respond, 'Oh, God, what are you still doing in bed?'" She was embarrassed by the situation. "I am a professional and part of what I sell is the mystique of professionalism. So if someone calls and wakes me up it's not too professional."

To avoid further incidents, Linda installed a phone answering machine, which she puts on to receive messages from 5:00 P.M. to 9:00 A.M. the next day. For many business owners who operate out of their home, an answering machine provides an important part of the boundary between work and home.

Although Linda's schedule has given her evening time to spend with Terry, they are often out of synch emotionally by the end of the day and on weekends. He spends a half hour in the morning on a commuter bus, eight hours in a high-pressured, hectic work environment, spends another half hour jammed into another crowded bus home, picks up his car, and arrives home wanting to be left alone to unwind.

Linda on the other hand, "comes home" to a place she never left. It takes her a half hour to shower, dress, and have a cup of coffee, and ten seconds to walk to her office. After eight hours of working in utter solitude—she can work with no interruptions if she chooses to put on the phone machine—she is glad to hear Terry's car pull into the driveway. When she opens the front door, she wants a hug and to talk. By Friday he is exhausted and looks forward to a quiet weekend of staying home. By Friday she is also exhausted but looks forward to a social weekend away from home, where she's been all week. They have had to recognize their different rhythms and try various compromises to make them fit together.

Linda has discovered that it is important for her to get out of the house during the week. She has had to force herself to do this.

Several nights a week, I make myself go to an exercise class at 5:30. It gets me out of the house and gives Terry time to unwind. I also try to schedule at least one or two meetings outside of the home every week, otherwise it gets too lonely, professionally as well as personally.

Terry, on the other hand, recognizes that Linda gets lonely, and that she needs and wants to talk, so they spend several hours each evening talking. He also makes an effort to go out with her at least one evening every weekend.

Linda's personality makes it difficult for her to work at home—she is not by nature a loner.

I have to have someone to talk to or to bounce ideas off of or I go bananas. I don't want to be a recluse. Maybe some people would enjoy that, but I don't. I am a very people-oriented person and I like to be with people, so sometimes it is hard to be in a room by myself.

Linda is willing to accept the difficulties of working at home for the advantage of controlling her own worklife. "I am happy doing what I do. I feel mentally stimulated, I am being paid for doing something that I really enjoy doing, and I am on my own. I don't know if a lot of people can say that they really enjoy their work."

Andrea Cannon

Andrea Cannon's story is one familiar to increasing numbers of women who advance to the lower rungs of management but discover, in their early forties, that they will go no further. The *Wall Street Journal* described them as living under a "glass ceiling"—they can see clearly to the top, but they can't get through.

Andrea Cannon worked for fifteen years—from 1964 to 1979—in church organizations. Her experiences were not all positive. "As a middle-management executive in nonprofit work, I found that I was the youngest woman executive, next to the top man of each group in which I worked. I was the hardest working person and yet I was the lowest paid, the youngest, and the newest." And the most vulnerable.

To cut costs, these organizations periodically eliminated positions, particularly at the middle-management level. As the newest person hired, Andrea was often one of the first people fired. Over the course of those fifteen years, she made a series of lateral moves from organization to organization, never really advancing in terms of title, responsibility, or pay. Eventually she decided it was time to get out of church work, seeing it was irredeemably "a man's world."

In 1980, she took a job as director of the evening program at the Berlitz School. Although she had a higher title than before, it was only a part-time job. She began to think seriously about how she could use her particular skills to earn more money. "I figured that you can't sell organization; you can't sell public speaking: and you can't sell idealism. So I said, 'I can type,' and I love typing." Like many good typists, Andrea truly enjoys her skill and likens typing to sculpting or painting. "I am not an artistic person, but to me typing is a form of creating something beautiful and at the same time it is practical and can help other people—all of which were important to me."

In 1979, she decided to start a typing business at home, while retaining her position at Berlitz. She would type in the morning and work at Berlitz in the afternoon and evening. She used her savings to buy a blue IBM Selectric typewriter, which she fondly referred to as The Blue Blaze, then consulted with the Chamber of Commerce's organization of retired executives about finding clients. Someone there suggested that she post 3 × 5 cards on the laundry-room bulletin board of her apartment building. "Since I live in a complex with ten buildings and each building has its own laundry room I took his advice. I started pulling in business and I couldn't believe it."

She discovered a guidebook for people interested in starting their own home typing business, a book that was both "cheerful and helpful," giving both practical suggestions and psychological ones. She used this book as the basis for starting the typing guild that later proved so helpful to Beth Stover. The guild was instrumental in the expansion of Andrea's business. "When anyone in the group had overload work or wanted to go on vacation, they would refer work to me. So they helped to keep me in business all those years I was only working part-time."

She began to set financial goals for herself—how much money she would make each month, how much by six months—and from her monthly records she could see that the business was rapidly growing. By 1983 she recognized that it was time to enter the computer age. She traded in The Blue Blaze and got an electronic typewriter with memory and some computerized electronic functions. Although not very sophisticated it was her introduction to computers.

The following year Andrea decided she had to make some hard decisions about her career.

I was forty-six and felt like my back was against the wall. I had to do something, but I didn't know what to do—whether to go full-time typing, whether to go full-time back into the corporate world, whether to go back into church work. But I had to do something if I was going to survive in my old age. I decided I wasn't cut out for the dog-eat-dog world of corporations, and that I had had it with the church organizations, so I decided to go with the typing.

By accident she discovered a word processor that could use her electronic typewriter as a printer. She took this as a confirming omen that she should make a full commitment to the typing. Although technologically equipped, she was still afraid of taking the risk, a fear she feels many women share.

Years ago, an older woman said to me that women do not go into business for themselves because they are afraid to take the chance. Her statement stuck in my mind. I think we women crave security and I think a lot of women cop out and make less than they can because they settle for security rather then running a risk.

To overcome her fear, she began to think about and talk to the women she had known over the years who had gone into business for themselves. One woman was a speech writer, one an accountant, another a typist, and others were musical and literary agents. She began to examine what they all had in common and how she measured up.

For one thing, they were all experienced. "Most of them were in their forties when they started their businesses. They had built up their skills and self-confidence. They knew that they had expertise in some area of their lives—whether at home or in a job." Secondly, they'd spent time examining the skills that made them successful, either in their families, or in the work world, or both. "All of them had developed their business using those skills to make money." Third, they all had some financial reserves, from inheritance, divorce, or savings. "They had a certain financial security to launch them and they didn't have other people financially dependent on them as, for example, a woman working to put her children through college might have." They could afford to take the risk.

Andrea was convinced she had all the necessary attributes. "Everything was there. I had self-confidence in my typing. I knew I could get along well with people. I had financial reserves that I had saved up through years and years of work. Beyond that I had a tremendous desire to achieve."

From the time Andrea was a young girl, she had admired women who achieved on their own—not by being the wife of someone, or the daughter of someone, but on their own. She herself had often had a nagging sensation that her accomplishments might be due to her father's success and reputation. "My father was very big in national church organizations. When I was working with these organizations I always wondered if I was being given an award or named to *Who's Who* because of my father." Perhaps because of that doubt her desire to achieve on her own was intense.

It is interesting that although Andrea had spent so much time in the midst of the private nonprofit world, her income was an important measure of her worth. "I always wanted to charge what I was worth." Starting a full-time home typing business was a way to test her worth. "In my church work and at Berlitz, I had a fixed salary. No matter how much I worked, I was limited financially by the salary structure of the organizations. It seemed to me that the sky was the limit if I worked on my own. I could make as little as I wanted or as much."

Part of her entrepreneurial spirit might have been inherited from her mother's side of the family. "I have a great-grandfather who started a very successful real estate company. His son started a department store in Philadelphia. There is definitely merchandising in my background, and temperamentally I enjoy selling." She translated the enjoyment of selling goods into the job of selling her typing skills and established specific goals for herself. She was very realistic about these goals, so as not to set herself up for failure.

"I said, 'I have got to make $300 a week,' and I gave myself three months to make it. I decided that if I made $300 a week within thirteen weeks, then I would set it higher. By the end of the thirteen weeks, I had almost doubled my initial goal." Within a year she had stabilized at $900 a week for 35 hours of work.

In the process of setting increasingly higher goals, Andrea had to set realistic work schedules. Unlike Linda, whose relationship with her husband made her keep her schedule under control, Andrea lives alone. In the early days, she had to force herself to quit working. Adrenaline coupled with anxiety could have led her to work around the clock in order to meet her quota. She quickly realized that such hours would only lead to burn-out, and put herself on a strict schedule to ensure that she worked reasonable hours.

She gets up every morning at 8:00, bathes, dresses, and has breakfast, then "leaves for her office" at 8:45. She has a daily ritual in which she leaves her apartment, walks around the block, and comes back in at 9:00 ready to work. She reverses the schedule in the evening. At 5:00 she turns on her answering machine and leaves her apartment to shop, run errands, or see friends.

She rarely works in the evening or on weekends, having discovered that she actually accomplishes more by limiting her work to a nine-to-five, Monday-through-Friday schedule. To prevent interruptions, she tries to limit her clients' visits. They drop off or pick up work by appointment and are not encouraged to wait in her apartment for the work.

Since she lives alone, she has to be careful about security, but has never had an incident, perhaps because she gets most of her clients by word of mouth from prior clients. She also trusts her instincts. If someone calls whose voice doesn't ring right, she will turn down the work. All of the women in our study who work at home with outside clients have at some point refused work for exactly that reason. Andrea does keep a knife in a drawer near her typewriter, but anticipates never having to use it.

Now approaching fifty, Andrea has come to terms with her various desires. The typing business did not completely satisfy all her ambitions, but she chose it because it has allowed her to achieve financial independence.

Robin Sanger

"I am a decision-type of person. I want to be in charge of my life. I didn't marry my husband to let him be in charge of my life. That's just my way—I'm headstrong." As a result of being headstrong and straightforward Robin Sanger, a twenty-seven-year-old computer programmer from a small Connecticut town, has been able to negotiate a changing series of work arrangements with one employer to suit her changing needs.

"I have worked the whole gamut. I have worked full-time in the office; I have worked part-time in the office, full-time at home and part-time at home. Right now part-time in the office with a little time at home seems to be the best." Robin is convinced that the reason she was successful in working out all of these agreements was that she was always straightforward and honest about what she wanted. "I have been upfront with my employer for a long time. They've always known where I've stood and I've always known where they stood. We've had a very good working relationship."

The women in this book so far have been self-employed, as are the vast majority of people who work in their homes, but Robin Sanger is an exception—she is a home-based employee for a Connecticut insurance company. Despite all of the current discussion about companies hiring people to work by computer out of their homes, the actual number of companies who hire people to do this is less than three hundred. Robin is both typical and atypical of this group.

She is typical insofar as she'd been a company employee before she worked at home. When she made the switch from the office to home, it was a result of a private agreement with her supervisor and it resulted in her status being changed to that of a self-employed contractor.

Several points are illustrated by Robin's experience. First, employers rarely hire people from outside their own company as home-based employees. If they hire people from outside they take them as independent contractors, not employees. Second, only a few companies—notably Mountain Bell and Pacific Bell—have formal home-based programs to which their employees can transfer. Most home-based employees have to work out individual agreements that apply only to them. Being allowed to work at home is generally awarded as a favor to a very valued employee whom the company wants to keep. Third, employers often change the status of their own workers when they transfer to home-based work. They cease being employees, with benefits and pensions, and become independent contractors without such coverage.

Robin is atypical in two ways. First, she always assumed that she could state her needs for her job and open the discussion for negotiation with her employer—a reflection of her headstrong and straightforward qualities. Second, she works for an amazingly open-minded company. There are thousands of employees across the nation who would love to work for an employer with the generosity and flexibility hers has. Her story is a tribute to both her abilities and the clearsightedness of her employer, who recognized that a happy employee would be a more productive one.

Robin started working for the insurance company when she was 21, after three years of college. She had had training in accounting and was hired in that department. She was a full-time employee there for four years, when, in 1981, she took maternity leave to have her daughter Eva.

"At the time I left, my job was such that they had to replace me. They couldn't leave the job open for six weeks. They promised that I would have a job when I returned, but that it wouldn't necessarily be that job. I said, 'Fine, I don't have a problem with that. I don't know after I have the baby whether I want to work part-time, full-time, or not at all.'" She had no idea about how she was going to feel once she gave birth and she also wanted to leave her options open.

After Eva was born, Robin went on maternity leave for two months. After that money ran out, she told the company that she needed to work a little bit, primarily for the extra money, but didn't want to leave her six-week-old baby in day-care. They asked her if she wanted to work at home. "I said, 'Well, okay, but doing what?' They didn't have a position in accounting for me, but they offered me a position in their computer department." Since she had no experience with computers, they offered to teach her and hired her back as an independent contractor to work at home forty hours a week on one of their personal computers.

The company wanted to automate their offices and needed someone to master the program. For the first six months she stayed home learning word processing. She grew increasingly dissatisfied with the home-based arrangement.

The reality did not match her fantasies, and she didn't like the independent contracting arrangement.

I thought working at home would be roses. It was a novelty, something I felt like bragging about. I felt really proud of myself that it could work out like this—I could be home with my child and have a job. I thought it would be easy to manage my time. If you've ever gone from working full-time to going home full-time, you think, Gosh, once I'm home I can do all these wonderful things. I can strip down my cabinets, and refinish the shelves, and all those things you just don't do when you're at work all day.

But she discovered that it sounded better than it was. "It might be the ideal arrangement for some people, but it wasn't for me. It just wasn't what it was cracked up to be. There were definite pros and cons to it. I thought there would only be pros and there weren't. I guess the grass always looks greener on the other side."

The hardest part for Robin was the lack of separation between her work and her family.

I have the kind of work that you can't pick up, put down, pick up, put down. When you have a child you have to pick it up and put it down. I can't do that. I have got to look at my program and concentrate and think about things; there's a lot of logic involved. You have to keep that logical frame and when you're constantly interrupted with "Give me a glass of water," it doesn't work. When you're working at home, you think, Oh, I should be washing the floor, and if you're washing the floor, you're thinking, Oh, I should be getting that job done. It is hard because there's no separation.

The lack of separation prompted her to discover more guilt than she had ever known. "I was always guilty and I got it both ways—if I was working, I felt guilty for not paying attention to my child; if I was with Eva I felt guilty for not doing my job. I was guilty either way I went."

She also found that she and her husband had little time together in the evening. "Dan would work all day and when he came home, I would say, 'Here is Eva,' and then I'd go to work." Like many home-based working women, Robin found that she did more of the housework once she was working at home than she had when she worked outside. "When I worked in the office, Dan and I shared a lot of responsibilities. But when I worked at home I was around more and I just did more."

She also had the common problem of her husband "forgetting" that she worked, since she worked at home.

I think that men have the feeling that when you're home all day long all you do is sit around and watch soap operas and eat bon-bons. There were a few days when I had to go into the office and he stayed home and watched Eva. He got bored, but that's because when he watched Eva he just watched her. When I watch Eva I also have to mop my floor and do the laundry. But he didn't, so he thought that when I was home all day, I had nothing to do but play with Eva.

She also quickly became disenchanted with her status as a contractor. The problem was not so much with what she got, but rather what she gave up when she lost her employee status. As an independent contractor she was paid $11.08 an hour and 20¢ a mile for travel expenses, plus her telephone expenses, which were considerable since she had to use the phone for electronic hookups to the computers and for conference-call meetings. But she lost the benefits of being an employee. Unlike many of the women who are hired as contractors, she knew exactly what was at stake. "When I was an independent contractor any income I earned was on a 1099 form, and therefore I had to pay self-employment tax. I had to pay my own Social Security and my employer paid nothing. When I was an employee, I put in a certain percent [7.15 percent] and my employer matched it. When I was a self-employed independent contractor, I paid 12.3 percent and my employer paid nothing." In addition she received no paid sick leave, no paid vacation time, and got no accrual to her pension plan, which had been 50 percent vested at the time that she went on maternity leave.

She'd lost both her job security and her sense of identity with the company. "As a contractor, I felt like the guy coming in from the outside, even though I had been there for so many years. I'd rather be an employee any day."

There came a point, when Eva was about a year old, when Robin decided she had had enough. "I didn't want to be at home full-time. I liked being with Eva, and I didn't want to work full-time, but I wanted to get out of the house."

Although she needed a change, she definitely wanted to keep working.

I like being paid for what I do. I take pride in what I do and I think I am respected for what I do and that means a lot to me. It is certainly nice when somebody is grateful for what you do. Unlike being a mother, which is an ungratifying job. You do a lot of things for a lot of people, and I don't begrudge that and I do it freely of my own will, but there is very little thanks involved. There is a lot of output for very little input. And it can wear on you and maybe that was why I didn't want to be home full-time.

She started going into the office one or two days a week, and became a part-time employee. This gave her both benefits and job security. "Plus I felt like more a part of the company as an employee. If there was a company picnic, or candlelight bowling, or a dinner to celebrate monthly sales, I was a part of it. As an employee I also got my own office. What more could I ask for?"

Money. As an employee she earned more. She had to pay less into Social Security, and got an hourly raise to $12.50 an hour. Given the years she had worked for the company, she also got three weeks of paid vacation, plus sick leave, and was once again back in the pension plan. After several years Robin was fully vested, as the company chose not to count her time as a contractor as a break in service, although technically it was.

When she became an employee again Robin got the company to let her work out an arrangement so that she works three days in the office and any additional time she wants at home.

Now that she earns $19,500 a year from her thirty-hour-a-week part-time job, she is satisfied. "As a part-timer how many people get paid what I get, have an office, have the benefits, and the flexibility? I must be doing something right or they wouldn't let me."

Psychologically she prefers working outside the home.

> When I go to work, it's my reputation. It's not my husband's reputation, it's not my family's. I think that a wife who is home all the time has only the status of her husband, and I don't work that way. I am not trying to be a woman's libber or anything. I'm not that. I don't think of myself that way, but my status is my status. Working outside the home has helped me get that for myself—my own self-image.

There are additional reasons why she prefers working at the office outside the home.

> I get out of the house. I can get more work done. When I worked at home, I didn't work when my child was awake or when she needed my attention. I've heard that a lot of people do that and that's fine for them, but my reason for being home was so I could spend time with my child. So therefore I worked when she was asleep or in the evenings when my husband came home. It was just too difficult trying to find the hours to work. I felt that the attention that my daughter needed was more important than working, so it was kind of ambiguous. Now I go into my office and I get my work done. I don't think about her and I don't think about the floor that needs to be washed. When I am at work, I don't think about home. When I am home I don't think about

work. It's like work is work and home is home. I find that when I work outside the home, I have less pressure on me, because I am only thinking of one thing. I am not thinking of twenty-five things.

She also prefers the social contacts of working, which she missed when she worked at home.

I enjoy the people I work with. It's like a relief in a lot of ways, talking to adults, and we're all talking about the same things. It's nice to talk to someone on an intelligent level instead of reading good-night stories. Also, I can rely on the knowledge of my workers. If I run into snags, they unsnag them. Whereas from home, it's hard to explain your snag over the phone.

Robin is convinced that for her type of work and her family situation working part-time outside the home is the ideal arrangement. "I'm very, very happy with my situation right now. I feel like I have the best of both worlds. I work three days a week in the office, and they can be any three days I want." One week, she may go in Monday, Wednesday, and Friday; another week Wednesday, Thursday, and Friday. "I can take my daughter on a picnic one day a week and really enjoy her and have her enjoy me."

There is clearly no one perfect way to work successfully at home. There is, however, a crucial attitude, and it is one of clarity, conviction, and willingness to negotiate. A woman who successfully works at home has to be clear with herself, with members of her family, and with her boss and clients about what she needs and what she expects. She also has to have the conviction that she deserves what she wants.

As we've seen, working at home raises numerous conflicts for women. If they are home, they feel they should do more of the housework. They feel they should consider themselves lucky, even if the arrangement doesn't suit them. Autonomy is achieved at the cost of isolation. Only if a person has the clarity of her conviction can she negotiate her way through these conflicts and create an acceptable situation.

Linda prefers working with people, but to have control of her work, she makes a trade-off. Robin loves working with people and was unwilling to give that up in order to work full-time. She felt no guilt or conflict about changing her mind when she realized that working at home full-time did not suit her needs. Women who are able to be clear about their needs and who are willing to renegotiate as their circumstances and needs change are most likely to make home-based work work for them.

7

Women and Home-based Work

Home-based work has a mixed reputation. On the one hand it is praised as an ideal work arrangement for a wide variety of people—a way for younger women to earn money and raise a family; for older women to reenter the labor force; for entrepreneurial women to start their own businesses. But on the other hand, people who do home-based work are given little credibility; they are not taken as seriously as those who work outside the home. There are many difficult aspects to this "ideal solution."

The intent in this book was to go beyond the rhetoric and hype about home-based work and find out what it really is like. What we've seen is that it is merely a job or career option which, like any other, has both advantages and disadvantages, and generates possibilities yet has limitations. The main advantages are flexibility, particularly in balancing work, family, and autonomy—the ability to work in your own way at your own pace. Yet "flexibility" and "autonomy" are to a certain extent euphemisms. Flexibility can be as much a curse as a blessing, and autonomy can result in isolation. Despite all the positive press about home-based work, the stories we've heard indicate that for many people the disadvantages are greater than the advantages.

The lack of credibility is a serious issue—perhaps more for the woman home-based worker, since a woman at home is there in the traditional roles of wife and mother. Family and friends are slow to understand that although she is "at home," she is really at work, and they often call, drop in, or make requests that they would never make of someone in an office.

Because of this problem women must set limits as to what family, friends, and clients can expect of them. It requires a woman to be definitive—to be able to say unequivocally "I cannot talk on the phone now." "I will not interrupt my work to run to the dry cleaners." "I cannot stop every few minutes for my child." An office or business environment is designed to make work possible. A home is not, so the entire physical and emotional support that makes it a work environment must be imposed deliberately. Many women find that difficult to do, especially because they find it hard to put limits on their availability as wives and mothers.

Yet if they can't set limits and create a work environment, they will have trouble separating their roles as mothers and homemakers from their roles as wage earners. The house itself constantly reminds them of what their homemaker selves could be doing—the floor has to be washed, the laundry folded, the checkbook balanced, the children's dentist appointments made. People constantly intrude.

To work effectively at home a work environment must be established and protected by distinct boundaries. Only certain hours can be worked; limits are put on housework or child care while you work; work is confined to one room and treated exactly as it would be in an office. Rules are necessary and must be made and kept.

Loneliness is another major problem. The suburbs are not what they were in the 1950s, when nearly two-thirds of all mothers stayed home. Today they are likely to be deserted from eight until five, since two out of every three mothers work outside the home. A home-based worker in a suburban neighborhood may find she is alone, and unless her work boundaries are clear, neighbors may assume she will pick up slack for them. Since she's "at home" everyone may expect her to help out at school, receive and sign for deliveries, or watch over neighborhood children whose parents are away at work.

The isolation bred by home-based work has been criticized by trade unions such as the AFL-CIO and International Ladies Garment Workers Union, who argue that it will lead to abuses of home-based workers. Because home workers are often cut off from information, the fear from the unions is that they will get paid less than they deserve and work longer than they should. There's also fear that they could end up putting their children to work. These criticisms have to be dealt with in a fair way. I have seen no evidence of child labor abuses among white-collar home workers, such as accountants, planners, typists, bookkeepers, or data entry clerks, but there is evidence of child labor in more manual or industrial types of home work. It is easy, however, to find evidence of hiring practices that are unfair if not actually illegal.

As things now stand companies can hire home workers as "independent contractors" but expect them to perform as if they were employees. This arrangement is better than none for many women typists, data entry clerks, and computer programmers, but it is not fair. They end up earning less than they would receive for doing the same work in an office, while the company saves on the average of 30 to 50 percent on each worker. These contractors work and live in isolation. Typically the company offers them no opportunity to learn additional skills or receive promotions. They are not part of the office social world, are not invited to holiday parties or events, and often do not even know the names of other women who do the same type of work. They have no way to compare how or what they are paid.

These conditions can make a home-based worker a kind of second-class corporate citizen—out of the mainstream, with no advancement opportunities and no job security. They could be terminated any time the workload declines. Since these women feel the precariousness of their positions, they are often afraid to speak up or complain for fear of being let go. They have come to believe that although they may provide valuable skills, they are expendable—they know that there are plenty of other mothers at home who would love to have their jobs.

A recent Congressional report on the pros and cons of clerical home work has questioned the legality of the "independent contractor" arrangement. In addition, a legal case in California challenges companies who hire workers on this basis. The unions and media make much of their concern that computers will make workers vulnerable to abuse. Their energies would be better spent advocating corporate hiring practices that ensure fair and equal treatment of workers regardless of where they work.

The isolation of home-based work is not merely emotional or social—not being part of a typical office culture deprives a woman of the practical and professional benefits of having colleagues. She will not get the kind of information one gathers informally in the lunchroom, the mailroom, or the bathroom—information about changes and developments in her line of work, ideas that could lead to new possibilities. A woman running a business out of her home may not keep abreast of changes in prices and rates and find herself undervalued in the marketplace. Those who run a home-based business can compensate for the lack of office culture by joining business groups, or trade guilds focused on their type of work, and can thus ensure that they have access to the kind of information they need.

Home-based work can be especially difficult for those who do not choose it as a positive act but were forced into it by circumstance. Ideally, career choices are made out of a sense of opportunity. Home-based work is often pursued because there was no other choice. For many the home is the workplace of last resort.

The lack of choice is often caused by the pressure of time. An expectant mother has only so long to decide how to combine work and children. A new mother who suddenly realizes that she can't leave her child and go back to her office job has even less time to make a new arrangement. A woman who has been fired, laid off, or suddenly abandoned by her husband may not have the peace of mind, the time, or the financial resources to consider carefully the alternatives, weigh different options, or create the ideal situation. The fact that institutions give so little support to working women provides further pressure. Pregnant women face limited opportunities for maternity leave—only four out of ten working women can take time off to have their children and keep their job.

Working parents have to deal with general and severe shortage of opportunities for child care. In 1986, nearly ten million children under the age of six had working mothers. About one and a half million of them were in licensed child care centers, while the other eight and a half million were in "unlicensed care," which means that the facilities or providers had never been reviewed by a public body to ensure the adequacy of their care. Of the eight and a half million in "unlicensed care," about four million were in family day-care homes, in which a neighborhood woman looks after children for a fee. The remaining four and a half million were cared for by baby-sitters, relatives, or play schools.

Not only is there not enough child care available, but what is available is very expensive. In-home care runs about $8,000 a year. Top quality care outside the home is estimated to be $5,000 a year, and acceptable care in licensed pre-schools averages $3,500.

Besides availability and cost, many find the scheduling of child care a problem. The lucky parents are the ones who have child care that coincides completely with their work hours. The vast majority of workers are not so fortunate and end up having to piece together a series of arrangements. A child care center may close so early that a parent who commutes can't get there in time, which means an additional arrangement for child care in that portion of the day has to be made. If either the child or the child care provider gets sick the parents are forced to scramble for alternatives, often requiring the woman to take time off from work—as evidenced by the higher rate of absenteeism for women than men. Arthur Emlen of Portland State University in Oregon interprets this decision as a "family response"—by increasing her own absenteeism, a woman protects the stability of her husband's job. The situation is improving slowly but parents ultimately need more cooperation from their employers. Dana Friedman of the Conference Board, a research organization for American businesses, estimates that in 1987 at least 3,000 companies offered some type of child care assistance—an increase from 600 in 1982. Most offer referral systems or financial assistance through flexible benefits programs, but approximately 200 corporations, 500 hospitals, and 50 government agencies have child care facilities on site. As important as child care services are, working parents also need more flexibility in the design and scheduling of jobs.

The majority of jobs in this country remain full time, Monday through Friday, nine-to-five jobs. Families have borne the stress of these rigid job structures. As it has become common for both parents to work and as more families are headed by a single parent, millions of children become "latchkey kids," coming home to empty houses. Millions more may absorb the effects of corporate decisions by staying in school twelve months a year or attending longer days. In other words, rather than forcing employers to rethink the ways jobs might best accommodate the changing needs of families, the responsibility for changes in our economy and culture have been thrust on parents and children. Parents who want to take time off while their children are young simply have to quit their jobs, gambling on their ability to get back into the job market or on their ability to switch to being self-employed.

Many parents, particularly mothers, turn to home-based work, sometimes under pressure, as the best alternative for raising their children and earning money. Although home-based work is an option, it can't be promoted as "the answer" to the problems of working and child care. Perhaps the next stage will be to recognize that the structure of work itself can be changed to benefit both parents and children.

It is clearly time for employers to explore other possibilities, and there are many. Some jobs could be made to coincide with conventional school schedules, running from September to June, 9:30 to 2:30. Full-time jobs could have part-time options during certain years of an employee's life, when parental needs come to the fore. Jobs could have "time off" options, so that the clock would stop running with regard to promotion, partnering, and other aspects of advancement. Workers who pursue these options should be able to do so without penalties.

In a culture where both men and women need to work, the needs of parenting should be of concern to everyone. A society that claims to value family life and children must acknowledge that good parenting is indispensable. Developing job structures that accommodate family needs would help balance the new division of responsibilities between parents.

Another reason for pursuing this is the fact that employers are wasting a tremendous labor pool of talented and ambitious women who at present see few ways to keep their jobs and raise their families. They often feel a tremendous allegiance to their employers, which is wasted when they are forced to quit. It seems wrong that so many women have so few options in the business world after they have children. To have skilled and experienced people forced to pursue work that does not utilize their talents is a national travesty. Home-based work offers an alternative in response to this problem, but for many, the work they do at home is less challenging, less important, and less lucrative than that which they did in the business world before they had children: They pay a penalty for having children.

Parents are not the only working people who turn to home-based work. As corporations increasingly cut their managerial staffs, more workers are displaced, many becoming free-lance consultants who work out of their homes. Others may come to feel blocked and eventually turn to a home-based business because they have better opportunities for advancement. In home-based work they see the opportunity to earn more money with more creativity and autonomy. Others find they are simply incapable of subordinating themselves to the demands, authority, or work-styles of an employer and would much rather work on their own, in their own way, at their own pace.

Despite all its difficulties, there are people who do home-based work who succeed and enjoy it. Some, particularly those without children, do better and go further than they ever would have with a conventional job. Those who succeed do so by successfully negotiating the many different kinds of agreements that have to be made. They have to negotiate with themselves over what kind of work they will do, what they expect to be paid for it, what hours they will work, and what kinds of relationships they will have with clients and employees. And they have to be clear with themselves that their work at home is serious work. They must treat it with respect and discipline.

Besides all this it is crucial for women to negotiate with their husbands over housework and child care. Women who work out of necessity must come to grips with the powerful image of the traditional woman and understand their own feelings about her privileges and responsibilities. By forfeiting the privilege of not working for pay, and assuming part of the responsibility of being a breadwinner, they have a right (and usually the necessity) of renegotiating the terms of housework and child care in their marriage. The terms of the new agreement must be made clear. In the process the woman has to realize that she is not being a bad wife and mother, but a fair and reasonable adult who expects equity in a relationship.

As we have seen, home work for most people turns out to be a stage in their life. For some it is a transition stage—while their children are young, or when they are trying to re-enter the job market after their children are grown. For others home-based work has nothing to do with their having children, and everything to do with having a degree of autonomy and creativity denied them in the conventional world of employees. Whatever the motivation for pursuing home-based work, if a person can be self-conscious, open, and alert to the need to continually revise and maintain the balance between one's work life and personal life, this way of working can be a positive career choice which generates opportunities and gives one power.

There are many more stories about home-based work that we have yet to hear. The stories in this book are of white, middle-class women who work at home. We have not heard from women of color, women newly arrived in the United States, women on public assistance, and women in religious communities. In the barrios of Spanish Harlem, the backrooms of Silicon Valley homes, and the lofts of Chinatown, women do back office data entry, assemble computer chip casings, and construct garments. In Chicago, a project is under way to provide assistance to those on public welfare to start their own home-based businesses. In central New Jersey efforts are being made to establish home-based work opportunities for orthodox Jewish women married to Talmudic scholars who, by necessity, are engaged in study rather than income-producing work. These disparate groups are each in a unique part of the culture, with some concerns and problems that are identical with those of the women in this book, and some which are special to their circumstances. Their stories are yet to be told.

8

The Next Stage

Much of this book has been about the unspoken contracts of women. The most deeply rooted one is that which she has with herself, forged in her childhood and influenced strongly by her parents. For women who live alone, this contract becomes the basis for her negotiation with herself regarding her hopes, dreams, and aspirations. For married women this same contract becomes the basis for many of the agreements, implicit and explicit, that she makes with her husband regarding what she hopes and wants for herself and for him. When the circumstances of her life necessitate change, some women have success in altering their agreements; others find that their initial terms are binding and inflexible.

If there is a single crucial lesson from the stories we have heard in this book, it is the fact that renegotiating the terms of these agreements requires a degree of openness and honesty that is distressingly rare. It is not so much that people want to avoid being open, as much as they want to avoid the pain that comes from scrutinizing areas never explored and perhaps changing roles and responsibilities established long ago. Yet by confronting and understanding the unspoken contracts that rule their lives many women have begun to articulate visions of what would better suit their needs.

The ideas that today's women hold regarding their work, their families, and their marriages have formed the focus of this book. Yet it is also clear that men have as many unspoken expectations for themselves and their wives as women do for themselves and their mates. It is time to let the man speak for himself—about his notion of marriage, his expectations for work, his dreams and frustrations. On the following pages, I have provided a survey designed for men who are either married or living with a women. It is time we heard from them.

National Survey of Men

Thank you for taking the time to answer this important national survey. Please mail your completed questionnaire to Dr. Kathleen Christensen, Graduate Center, City University of New York - Room 545, 33 West 42nd Street, New York, New York 10036.

(Please ignore any of the small numbers in parentheses or side columns; they are for tabulation only.)

SECTION I WORK EXPERIENCE

1–6

1. How do you identify your primary occupation? (Check only one.)

7–8

- *(01)* ___ business owner
- *(02)* ___ manager/official/officer
- *(03)* ___ professional
- *(04)* ___ technical
- *(05)* ___ sales
- *(06)* ___ clerical
- *(07)* ___ service

- *(08)* ___ craftsman; handyman
- *(09)* ___ blue collar
- *(10)* ___ homemaker full-time
- *(11)* ___ student
- *(12)* ___ unemployed
- *(13)* ___ retired
- *(14)* ___ other_____

2. Please describe your primary job.

_____

9–10

_____

_____

3. In your primary job are you:

11

- *(1)* ___ employed by a company or another person?
  ___ self-employed (if so, please check off your status):
- *(2)* ___ sole proprietorship
- *(3)* ___ partnership
- *(4)* ___ incorporated
- *(5)* ___ other_____

4. Do you have a second job? *(1)* ___ Yes   *(2)* ___ No   *12*

5. If yes, why do you have a second job? (Check all that apply.)

(13) ___ to earn extra money for now   *13–21*
(14) ___ to save money for the future
(15) ___ to start up my own business
(16) ___ to have more flexibility in my life
(17) ___ to learn another skill or trade
(18) ___ it's the kind of work I love
(19) ___ if I work a second job my wife doesn't have to take a paying
            job outside the home
(20) ___ preparing for a career change
(21) ___ other_____

6. How many hours a week do you work for pay? Job 1 _____   *22–23*

                                                  Job 2 _____   *24–25*

                                                  Job 3 _____   *26–27*

7. How many hours do you work on an unpaid basis?

                                                  Job 1 _____   *28–29*

                                                  Job 2 _____   *30–31*

                                                  Job 3 _____   *32–33*

8. When you were about 18 to 20 years old, did you have expectations
for what kind of work you wanted to do to earn a living?

(1) ___ Yes (If yes, go to question 9.)   *34*
(2) ___ No (If no, go to question 10.)

9. How well have your work experiences matched your expectations?

(1) ___ I have about what I wanted in my work   *35*
(2) ___ I have more than I ever expected
(3) ___ I have less than I expected in my work

10. In light of what you now know about job opportunities, would you have made different decisions when you were younger?

(1) _____ (If yes, go to question 11.)   36
(2) _____ (If no, go to question 12.)

11. What kinds of decisions would you make differently?

_____   37–40

_____

12. In making your decisions about a job, which is the most important factor? (Please check all that apply):

(41) _____ to earn as much money as I possibly can   41–44
(42) _____ to have a job that I feel is enjoyable or challenging
(43) _____ to have a job that I feel makes a contribution to society
(44) _____ to survive and have the rest of my time to enjoy other interests

13. Please circle the number in the list above which is your most impor-   45–46
tant reason for working.

14. What is your marital status?

(1) _____ married living with spouse   47
(2) _____ separated, divorced, widowed
(3) _____ single (never married)
(4) _____ single (living with partner)

(If you are married, go to question 15. If you are not married but living with a partner, go to section IV, question 50. If you are separated, divorced, widowed, or single, please go to question 53.)

SECTION II YOUR MARRIAGE

15. How old were you when you were married for the first time? _____   48–49

16. Is this your first marriage? *(50–1)* _____ Yes   *(2)* _____ No   50–51
If no, which is it? *(51)*_____

17. Is this your wife's first marriage? *(52–1)* ____ Yes   *(2)* ____ No   52–53
If no, which is it? *(53)*____

18. How many years have you been married to your present wife?____   54–55

19. All of the following questions pertain to your current marriage. Please check all the ways that you and your wife spend time together during a typical week.

(56) ____ We cook dinner together   56–69
(57) ____ We watch TV
(58) ____ We talk about the day
(59) ____ We go out to dinner
(60) ____ We run errands
(61) ____ We clean the house
(62) ____ We make love
(63) ____ We play with our children
(64) ____ We visit friends or family
(65) ____ We go bowling, play golf, or do other sports
(66) ____ We go shopping
(67) ____ We go to the movies
(68) ____ We go to church or synagogue activities
(69) ____ Other_____

20. When you got married did you expect to work for pay?

(70–1) ____ Yes   Why? *(71–72)* _____   70

_____   71–72

(2) ____   No   Why not? *(73–74)* _____   73–74

_____

21. When you got married did you expect your wife to work for pay?

(75–1) ____ Yes   Why? *(76–77)* _____   75

_____   76–77

(2) ____   No   Why not? *(78–79)* _____   78–79

_____

22. Does your wife currently work for pay?

(1) ____ Yes (If yes, go to question 23.)   *80*
(2) ____ No (If no, go to question 24.)

23. Please describe your wife's current paying job(s).

Job 1. *(81–82)* _____
Hours worked per week. *(83–84)* ____   *81–84*

Job 2. *(85–83)* _____
Hours worked per week. *(87–88)* ____   *85–88*

24. During a typical week what household chores are *you* primarily responsible for? (Please check all that apply.)

(89) ____ Preparing and planning meals   *89–97*
(90) ____ Grocery shopping
(91) ____ Vacuuming
(92) ____ Taking out the garbage
(93) ____ Washing dinner dishes
(94) ____ Cleaning the bathroom
(95) ____ Doing the laundry
(96) ____ Running errands to the store
(97) ____ Other_____

25. Who in your family has overall responsibility for housework? (Please check only one.)

(1) ____ I do   *98*
(2) ____ My wife and I share it
(3) ____ My wife does
(4) ____ The children and I share it
(5) ____ The housekeeper or maid does
(6) ____ Other_____

26. How do you feel about your housework arrangement? (Please check the *one* that best applies.)

(1) ____ I'm fine with it   *99*
(2) ____ I would like to be able to do more
(3) ____ I would like my wife to do more

(Responses continued on next page)

(4) —— I would like my children to do more
(5) —— I would like to hire a housekeeper or maid
(6) —— Other _____

27. When you got married did you have specific expectations of what marriage would be like?

(1) —— Yes (If yes, go to question 28.)   *100*
(2) —— No (If no, go to question 29.)

28. In what ways has your marriage matched your expectations? In what ways has it not matched them?

_____   *101–104*

_____

29. How satisfied are you with your love life?

(1) —— very satisfied   *105*
(2) —— somewhat satisfied
(3) —— satisfied
(4) —— somewhat dissatisfied
(5) —— very dissatisfied

30. Approximately how often do you and your wife make love?

(1) —— every day   *106*
(2) —— a few times a week
(3) —— once a week
(4) —— a few times a month
(5) —— once a month or less

31. Which statement do you believe best describes your attitude? (Check only one.)

(1) —— The person who makes the most money in a marriage   *107*
should have the greatest say in making decisions.
(2) —— Money makes no difference in how decisions are made.
(3) —— Money should make no difference in how decisions get made but it does.

32. Please look over the following topics. For each topic, please check if you and your wife agree about the topic, disagree, or never talk about it.

	We agree	We disagree	We never talk about this	
Your plans for the future	*(1)* ___	*(2)* ___	*(3)* ___	108
The type of social life you want as a couple with other people	*(1)* ___	*(2)* ___	*(3)* ___	109
The amount of time the two of you should spend alone with one another	*(1)* ___	*(2)* ___	*(3)* ___	110
How much money you should earn	*(1)* ___	*(2)* ___	*(3)* ___	111
How much money she should earn	*(1)* ___	*(2)* ___	*(3)* ___	112
How much money you spend for yourself	*(1)* ___	*(2)* ___	*(3)* ___	113
How much money she spends for herself	*(1)* ___	*(2)* ___	*(3)* ___	114
The amount of time you should spend together as a family	*(1)* ___	*(2)* ___	*(3)* ___	115
Who should take care of the children	*(1)* ___	*(2)* ___	*(3)* ___	116
Your love life	*(1)* ___	*(2)* ___	*(3)* ___	117
Your responsibilities to your and her parents	*(1)* ___	*(2)* ___	*(3)* ___	118
Who should cook evening meals	*(1)* ___	*(2)* ___	*(3)* ___	119
Who should shop for food	*(1)* ___	*(2)* ___	*(3)* ___	120
Who should clean the house	*(1)* ___	*(2)* ___	*(3)* ___	121
Whether she should work outside the home	*(1)* ___	*(2)* ___	*(3)* ___	122
Other_____	*(1)* ___	*(2)* ___	*(3)* ___	123

33. If there are areas in your marriage you would like to talk about, what are they and why can't you talk about them?

_____   *124–130*

_____

34. If you could create your own dream life, what would it be like?

_____   *131–135*

_____

_____

35. How old are you? _____   *136–137*

36. How old is your wife? _____   *138–139*

37. What do you earn annually? _____   *140–145*

38. What does your wife earn annually? _____   *146–151*

39. What is your wife's educational level?

   (1) ___ some high school   *152*
   (2) ___ high school graduate
   (3) ___ some college (less than four years)
   (4) ___ college graduate
   (5) ___ post-college
   (6) ___ specialized training   please describe_____

40. If your wife earns more than you, how do you feel about that?

_____   *153–154*

_____

41. Overall, how satisfied are you with your marriage?

   (1) ___ very satisfied   *158*
   (2) ___ somewhat satisfied

(Responses continued on next page)

(3) ___ satisfied
(4) ___ somewhat dissatisfied
(5) ___ very dissatisfied   Why? _____   *159–162*

If you have children living with you, go to question 42.
If you don't have children living with you, go to question 53.

SECTION III   YOUR CHILDREN

42. Please list the ages of the children who live with you.

_____ _____ _____ _____ _____ _____   *163–176*

43. In the above list, please circle the ones from your present marriage.   *177–190*

44. Please check all the ways *you* most often spend time with your children during the week.

(191) ___ We spend time alone at home, playing and talking   *191–205*
(192) ___ We spend time with other children
(193) ___ We watch TV together at home
(194) ___ We go to the playground and play together
(195) ___ We run errands
(196) ___ We do our separate things
(197) ___ We read or play games at home
(198) ___ We go shopping together
(199) ___ I drop them off and pick them up
(200) ___ We go to the playground and I watch them play
(201) ___ Other parents and I work out arrangements to watch each other's children
(202) ___ My wife, children, and I do things outside the home together
(203) ___ We play sports
(204) ___ We go to watch sports events
(205) ___ Other _____

45. Who has primary responsibility for arranging the day-to-day care of your children? (Please check only one.)

(Responses continued on next page)

(1) ____ I do

206

(2) ____ my wife does

(3) ____ my wife and I share it on a roughly equal basis

(4) ____ the child-care provider does

(5) ____ other _____

46. How satisfied are you with being a father?

    (1) ____ very satisfied

207

    (2) ____ somewhat satisfied

    (3) ____ satisfied

    (4) ____ somewhat dissatisfied

    (5) ____ very dissatisfied

47. In what ways are you satisfied or dissatisfied? _____

208–210

_____

48. Do you think you spend enough time with your children?

    (1) ____ Yes (If yes, go to question 53.)

211

    (2) ____ No (If no, go to question 49.)

49. If no, would you consider any of the following arrangements in order to have more time with your children? (Please check all options you'd consider *if* you could financially afford it.)

    (212) ____ I'd organize my time better

212–217

    (213) ____ I'd switch to part-time work and have my wife work part-time

    (214) ____ I'd quit my job and stay home and let my wife work full-time

    (215) ____ I'd switch to part-time work and have my wife work full-time

    (216) ____ I'd start my own business so I could control my hours more

    (217) ____ other _____

(Please go to question 53.)

SECTION IV COUPLES LIVING TOGETHER

50. How long have you been living with your partner?_____ *218–219*

51. Do you intend to marry one another? *220*
(220–1) ____ Yes Why? _____ *221–223*
(2) ____ No Why not? _____ *224–226*

52. Do you consider that you are living now as husband and wife?

(1) ____ Yes (If yes, please return to Question 15 and complete *227*
questions 15–41 as if you were man and wife.)

(2) ____ No (If no, please go to next question.)

SECTION V BACKGROUND INFORMATION

53. What is your educational level?

(1) ____some high school *228*
(2) ____high school graduate
(3) ____some college (less than 4 years)
(4) ____college graduate
(5) ____post-college
(6) ____specialized training

54. What is your zip code?_____ *229–233*

55. Please record today's date. _____ _____ *234–237*
Month   Year

56. In order to contribute to a better understanding of men and their *238*
lives, would you be willing to be interviewed in more detail? If so,
please give us your name, address, and telephone number.

Name:_____

Address:_____

Telephone:_____

57. Is there anything you would like to mention that we left out of the questionnaire?

239–255

_____

_____

_____

Bibliography

A special report: The corporate woman. 24 March 1986. *Wall Street Journal*.

Ansberry, C. 7 August 1985. Feast or famine: Managers facing a wide disparity in job openings. *Wall Street Journal*.

Atkinson, W. November 1985. Telecommuter blues. *Management World*.

Bailyn, L. 1970. Career and family orientations of husbands and wives in relation to marital happiness. *Human Relations* 23: 97-113.

Beck, J. 6 August 1986. Women who fall off the fast track. *New York Daily News*.

Bloom-Feshbach, S., Bloom-Feshbach, J., and Heller, K. 1982. Work, family, and children's perceptions of the world. In Kamerman, S., and Hayes, C., eds., *Families that work: Children in a changing world*. Washington, D.C.: National Academy Press.

Boris, E. 18 October 1986. A woman's place. *Nation*.

———. March 1985. Regulating industrial homework: The triumph of "sacred motherhood." *Journal of American History* 71: 745-63.

Bronfenbrenner, U., and Crouter, A. 1982. Work and family through time and space. In Kamerman, S., and Hayes, C., eds., *Families that work: Children in a changing world*. Washington, D.C.: National Academy Press.

Brooks, A. 27 February 1984. When her office is at home. *New York Times*.

Butler, J., and Getzels, J. October 1985. *Home occupation ordinances*. Report 391. Chicago: American Planning Association.

Chafe, W. 1976. Looking backward in order to look forward: Women, work and social values in America. In Kreps. J., ed., *Women and the American economy: A look to the 1980's*. Englewood Cliffs, N.J.: Prentice-Hall.

Children's Defense Fund. 1982. *Employers, parents and their children: A data book*. Washington, D.C.: Children's Defense Fund.

Christensen, K. December 1985. Impacts of computer mediated home-based work on women and their families. Final report to the Office of Technology Assessment, U.S. Congress, for their study Automation of America's Offices, 1985-2000. Washington, D.C.: U.S. Printing Office, OTA-CIT-287.

————. 1988. The new era of home-based work. Boulder, Colorado: Westview Press.

————. 1985. Women and home-based work. *Social Policy* 15: 54-57.

————. 26 February 1986. Pros and cons of clerical homework. Testimony before the Employment and Housing Subcommittee, Committee on Government Operations, U.S. House of Representatives, Washington, D.C.

————. 1987. Women and contingent work. *Social Policy* 17: 15-18.

Churchman, D. 21 November 1983. Welcome home—fresh, vocal support for at-home mothers. *Christian Science Monitor*.

Clendinen, D. 2 December 1983. Court ban on work at home brings gloom to knitters in rural Vermont. *New York Times*.

Collins, E. G. C. 1986. A company without offices. *Harvard Business Review* 64: 127-36.

Collins, G. 20 March 1986. More women are retiring, and doing better. *New York Times*.

————. 3 April 1986. As more men retire early, more women work longer. *New York Times*.

Consultants may be the way to avoid "peak and valley" problems. 1986. *Infosystems* 33: 16.

Cook, B. E., and Rothberg, D. S. 1985. *Employee benefits for part-*

timers. McLean, Virginia: Association of Part-time Professionals, Inc.

Costello, C. 1985. On the front: Class, gender, and conflict in the insurance workplace. Ph.D. dissertation, University of Wisconsin.

————. 1986. "The office homework program of the Wisconsin Physicians' Insurance Company." Unpublished manuscript. New York: Russell Sage Foundation.

Cummings, J. 6 May 1986. Child care and business, side by side. *New York Times*.

Dahl, J. 19 May 1986. A special report: Small business; opening the financial door. *Wall Street Journal*.

Derow, E. O. 1977. Married women's employment and domestic labor. Ph.D. dissertation, University of Toronto.

De Sanctis, G. October 1983. A telecommuting primer. *Datamation* 29: 215-20.

Devanna, M. A. 1984. *Male/female careers: The first decade*. New York: Report for the Center for Research in Career Development, Columbia University, Graduate School of Business.

Diebold Automated Office Program. 1981. *Office work in the home: Scenarios and prospects for the 1980's*. New York: Diebold Group, Inc.

Dolinar, L. 14 February 1985. Working at home: A choice location. *Newsday*.

Eberhardt, B. J., and Shani, A. B. 1984. The effects of full-time vs. part-time employment status on attitudes toward specific organizational characteristics and overall job satisfaction. *Academy of Management Journal* 27: 893-900.

Economic Policy Council of UNA-USA, Family policy panel. 1985. Work and family in the United States: A policy initiative.

Ehrenhalt, S. M. 15 August 1986. Work force shifts in the 80's. *New York Times*.

Ehrenreich, B. 7 September 1986. Is the middle class doomed? *New York Times Magazine*.

Ehrlich, E., and M. A. Pollock. 25 August 1986. 9 to 5, and then some: More women are moonlighting. *Business Week*.

Emlen, A. 1984. "Hard to find and difficult to manage: The effects of child care on the workplace." Paper presented at forum on Child Care and Employee Productivity: The Workforce Partnership, at the Westin-Benson Hotel, Portland, Oregon.

Engstrom, M., Paavonen, H., and Sahlberg, B. 1986. *Tomorrow's work in today's society.* Stockholm: Swedish Council for Building Research.

Feld, S. 1963. Feelings of adjustment. In Nye, F. I. and Hoffman, L. W., eds., *The employed mother in America.* Chicago: Rand McNally.

Flexible high-flyers. 1984. *Economist 292/:* 71.

Foderaro, L. W. 21 August 1986. Working women speak out on home design. *New York Times.*

Forgang, I. 18 March 1986. Secretaries complain they feel under-utilized, isolated. *Wall Street Journal.*

Freudenberger, H. J. 1985. Women's burnout: How to detect and prevent it. *The Independent Practitioner* 5: 11-16.

Freund, Y. R. 4 June 1986. A New York City kind of cottage industry. *New York Times.*

Fuchs, V. R. 1986. Sex differences in economic well-being. *Science* 232: 432-64.

Galante, S. P. 16 June 1986. Employers face higher costs as Congress mandates benefits. *Wall Street Journal.*

————. 2 June 1986. Cottage businesses help ease farm-belt economy burdens. *Wall Street Journal.*

Gillette, A. 24 November 1983. Cottage trade could fill directory—and does. *Detroit News.*

Giovanni, J. 20 September 1984. Planning new living spaces for the non-traditional family. *New York Times.*

Glaser, B., and Strauss, A. 1967. *The discovery of grounded theory: Strategies for qualitative research.* Chicago: Aldin.

Goleman, D. 2 February 1986. The psyche of the entrepreneur. *New York Times Magazine.*

Gordon, G. E. 1986. *Putting your PC to work at home.* Monmouth Junction, N.J.: Gil Gordon Associates.

Gottlieb, D., and Dede, C. 1984. *The social role of the computer: implications for familial mental health.* Houston: Center for Public Policy.

Gove, W. R., and Geerken, M. R. 1977. The effect of children and employment on the mental health of married men and women. *Social Forces,* 56: 66-76.

Greer, W. R. 19 March 1986. Women now the majority in professions. *New York Times.*

Gregg, G. 1985. Women entrepreneurs: The second generation. *Across the Board* 22: 10-20.

———. 13 April 1986. Putting kids first. *New York Times Magazine.*

Gregory, J. 1983. The future: Clerical workers. Paper presented to National Executive Forum on Office Work Stations in the Home, National Academy of Science, Washington, D.C.

Gregory, J. and Nussbaum, K. 1982. Race against time: Automation of the office. *Office: Technology and People* 1(23): 197-236.

Hamel, H. R. 1985. New data series on involuntary part-time work. *Monthly Labor Review* 108: 42-43.

Harkness, R. C. 1977. *Technology assessment of telecommunications/transportation interactions.* Menlo Park, Calif.: Stanford Research Institute.

Hatsopoulos, G. N. 14 May 1986. Productivity lag is real trade barrier. *Wall Street Journal.*

Haw, M. 1982. Women, work and stress: A review and agenda for the future. *Journal of Health and Social Behavior* 23: 132-44.

Hayward, D. G. 1977. Psychological concepts of home among urban middle class families with children. Ph.D. diss. City University of New York.

Herbers, J. 13 May 1986. Rising cottage industry stirring concern in U.S. *New York Times.*

Hirshey, G. 5 November 1985. How women feel about working at home. *Family Circle.*

Horvath, F. W. 1986. Work at home: New findings from the current population survey. *Monthly Labor Review* 109 : 31-35.

Horwitz, J. 1986. Working at home and being at home: the interaction of microcomputers and the social life of households. Ph.D. dissertation. Graduate School, City University of New York.

Horwitz, J. and Tognoli, J. 1982. Role of home in adult development: Women and men living alone describe their residential histories. *Family Relations* 31: 335-41.

Howe, W. J. 1986. Temporary help workers: Who they are, what jobs they hold. *Monthly Labor Review* 109: 45-47.

Hunt, A. R. 6 June 1986. What working women want. *Wall Street Journal.*

Huws, U. 1984. *The new homeworkers.* London: Low Pay Unit.

If home is where the worker is. 3 May 1982. *Business Week.*

Jacobs, S. L. 15 April 1985. Partnerships are easy to start but not easy to keep going. *Wall Street Journal.*

————. 19 August 1985. Women owners, bankers argue over loan-bias allegations. *Wall Street Journal.*

————. 19 August 1986. Small-business conferences voice worries about impact of overhaul. *Wall Street Journal.*

Johnson, R. 29 June 1983. Rush to cottage computer work falters despite advent of inexpensive technology. *Wall Street Journal.*

Johnson, S. June 1985. The three-day work week: Making it work. *Working Woman.*

Kamerman, S. B. 1980. *Parenting in an unresponsive society: Managing work and family.* New York: Free Press.

Kamerman, S. B., and Hayes, C. D., eds. 1982. *Families that work: Children in a changing world.* Washington, D.C.: National Academy Press.

Kanter, R. M. 1977. *Work and family in the United States: a critical review and agenda for research and policy.* New York: Russell Sage Foundation.

Kantrowitz, B. et al. March 1986. A mother's choice. *Newsweek.*

Klott, G. 18 August 1986. Impact on individuals to stretch far beyond. *New York Times.*

Kotlowitz, A. 30 March 1987. Working at home while caring for a child sounds fine—in theory. *Wall Street Journal.*

Kraut, R. and Gambsch, P. Home-based, white-collar work: lessons from the 1980 census. *Social Force.*

Kreps, J. and Leaper, J. 1976. Homework, market work and the allocation of time. In J. Kreps, ed., *Women and the American economy: A look to the 1980's.* Englewood Cliffs, N.J.: Prentice-Hall.

Labor letter: A special news report on people and their jobs in offices, fields and factories. 3 December 1985. *Wall Street Journal.*

Langway, L. et al. 9 January 1984. "Worksteaders" clean up. *Newsweek*.

Larson, E. 13 February 1985. Working at home: Is it freedom or a life of flabby loneliness? *Wall Street Journal*.

Lawren, B. 1984. Working at home. *Woman's World* 5: 6-7.

Lawson, C. 1 August 1985. Aid for women starting businesses. *New York Times*.

Leidner, R. 1987. Home work: A study in the interaction of work and family organization. In I. Simpson and R. Simpson, eds., *Research in the sociology of work*. Greenwich, Ct.: JAI Press.

Lovenheim, B. March 1984. Stay at home and work. *Redbook*.

Lublin, J. S. 28 May 1985. Female owners try to make life easier for employees—sometimes too easy. *Wall Street Journal*.

Marenghi, C. 20 March 1984. Will telecommuting take hold? *PC Week*.

————. 1986. Managing New York options. *Infosystems* 33: 92.

Mattera, R. 2 April 1983. Home computer sweatshops. *The Nation*.

Matthaei, J. A. 1986. *An economic history of women in America*. New York: Schocken Books.

Max, S. 27 August 1986. The need for parental leaves. *New York Times*.

McClintock, C. 1981. Working alone together: Managing telecommuting. Department of Human Service Studies, Cornell University.

McLaughlin, M. A. 1981. Physical and social support systems used by women engaged in home-based work. Master's thesis, Cornell University.

Memmott, M. 15 July 1986. Temps finding a permanent niche. *USA Today*.

Michelson, W. 1981. Spatial and temporal dimensions of child care. In C. Stimpson et al., eds., *Women and the American city*. Chicago: University of Chicago Press.

Mitchell, C. 26 June 1986. Businesswomen say credit firms still discriminate on basis of sex. *Wall Street Journal*.

————. 19 February 1986. Desire to work at home gains popularity as motive for buying a personal computer. *Wall Street Journal*.

Moore, K., and Sawhill, I. 1976. Implications of women's employment for home and family life. In J. Kreps, ed., *Women and the American economy: A look to the 1980's.* Englewood Cliffs, N.J.: Prentice-Hall.

Morrisroe, P. January 1984. Living with the computer. *New York.*

Murray, A. 8 August 1986. Tax overhaul likely to increase the envy salaried workers feel for self-employed. *Wall Street Journal.*

Myers, H. F. 22 September 1986. The growth in services may moderate cycles. *Wall Street Journal.*

National Academy of Sciences. 1983. *Office workstations in the home.* National Executive Forum. Washington, D.C.

Near, J., Rice, R., and Hunt, R. 1981. The relationship between work and non-work domains: A review of empirical research. *Academy of Management Review* 5: 415-29.

New York State Council on Children and Families. 1983. *Part-time employment: Implications for families and the workplace.*

Nicholson, T. et al. 4 May 1981. Commuting by computer. *Newsweek.*

Nilles, J. 1982. *Exploring the world of the personal computer.* Englewood Cliffs, N.J.: Prentice-Hall.

Nilles, J., Carlson, F., Gray, P., and Hanneman, G. 1976. *The telecommunications–transportation tradeoff.* New York: Wiley.

Nixon, M. 5 January 1983. Home is where their office is: The rise of cottage industries. *USA Today.*

Noble, K. B. 11 May 1986. Commuting by computer remains largely in the future. *New York Times.*

———. 20 August 1986. U.S. weighs end to ban on factory homework. *New York Times.*

Olmsted, B. 1983. Changing times: The use of reduced work time options in the United States. *International Labour Review* 122: 479-92.

Olson, M. H. 1983. Remote office work: Changing work patterns in space and time. *Communications of the ACM* 26(3), 182-87.

Olson, M. H. and Primps, S. 1984. Working at home with computers: Work and nonwork issues. *Journal of Social Issues* 40: 97-112.

Otten, A. L. 25 September 1986. Deceptive picture: If you see families staging a comeback, it's probably a mirage. *Wall Street Journal.*

Pear, R. 27 August 1986. Poverty rate down slightly in 1985, to level of '81. *New York Times.*

Pleck, J. H. 1977. The work–family role system. *Social Problems* 24: 417-27.

Pollack, A. 26 May 1986. Home-based work stirs suit. *New York Times*.

———. 12 March 1981. Rising trend of computer age: Employees who work at home. *New York Times*.

Porter, S. 20 March 1986. Pensions go to work for women—finally. *New York Daily News*.

Pratt, J. 1984. Home teleworking: A study of its pioneers. *Technological Forecasting and Social Change* 25: 1-14.

Pratt, J. H., and Davis, J. A. 1986. *Measurement and evaluation of the populations of family-owned and home-based businesses*. Report to Small Business Administration.

Radloff, L. 1975. Sex differences in depression. *Sex Roles* 1: 249-65.

Reibstein, L. 18 April 1986. More companies use free-lancers to avoid cost, trauma of layoffs. *Wall Street Journal*.

———. 16 September 1986. To each according to his needs: Flexible benefits plan gains favor. *Wall Street Journal*.

Riseman, R., and Tomaskovic-Devey, D. 1986. The social construction of technology: Microcomputers and the organization of work. Unpublished manuscript.

Roberts, S. V. 8 October 1986. Of women and women's issues. *New York Times*.

Rose, A. M. 1955. Factors associated with life satisfaction of middle-aged persons. *Marriage and Family Living* 17: 15-19.

Rothschild, B. S. 14 April 1986. Parents get help juggling home, work. *USA Today*.

Saegert, S., and Winkel, G. 1979. The home: A critical problem for changing sex roles. *New Space for Women*. Boulder, Colorado: Westview Press.

Salomon, I., and Salomon, M. 1984. Telecommuting: The employee's perspective. *Technological Forecasting and Social Change* 25: 15-28.

Schmitt, E. 18 August 1986. Female entrepreneurs now own 25% of small businesses. *New York Times*.

Shirley, S. January-February 1986. A company without offices. *Harvard Business Review* 1: 127-36.

Shreve, A. March 1985. The maternity backlash: Women vs. women. *Working Woman.*

Silk, L. 8 January 1986. Automation's labor impact. *New York Times.*

———. 10 September 1986. Underground's hidden income. *New York Times.*

Slade, M. 21 October 1985. Working at home: The pitfalls. *New York Times.*

Sorenson, L. November 1984. How to work part-time. *Working Woman.*

Special Labor Force Reports. 1981. Working mothers and their children. *Monthly Labor Review* 104: 49-54.

Stalland, K., Ehrenreich, B., and Sklar, H. 1983. *Poverty in the American dream: Women and children first.* New York: Institute for New Communications.

State of New York, Department of Labor. 1982. Report to the governor and the legislature on the garment manufacturing industry and industrial homework. Albany, New York.

Stephen, B. 16 July 1986. Mother's helper. *New York Life.*

Stevens, M. January 1986. Seven common mistakes small businesses make and how to avoid them. *Working Woman.*

Stinson, J. F., Jr. 1986. Moonlighting by women jumped to record highs. *Monthly Labor Review.* 109: 22-25.

Szalai, A. et al. 1972. *The use of time: Daily activities of urban and suburban populations in twelve countries.* The Hague: Mouton Press.

Taylor, S., Jr. 30 November 1983. U.S. Court reinstates rules on "industrial" home work. *New York Times.*

Tepper, T., and Tepper, N. 1980. *The new entrepreneurs: Women working from home.* New York: Universe Books.

Tetlow, K. 1984. Home as the workplace within the setting of the bed and breakfast home. Unpublished paper, Center for Human Environments, Graduate Center, City University of New York.

Toffler, A. 1980. *The third wave.* New York: William Morrow.

U.S. Congress, House. 1983. *Family Opportunity Act.* 98th Cong. H.R. 2531.

U.S. Congress, House. 1986. Subcommittee of the Committee on Government Operations, Testimony on the pros and cons of home-based clerical work.

U.S. Congress, Office of Technology Assessment. December 1985. Automation of America's offices. Washington, D.C.: U.S. Government Printing Office, OTA-CIT-287.

U.S. Department of Labor, Bureau of Labor Statistics. 1986. Women in the American labor market: Continuity and change.

U.S. Department of Labor. 1986. BLS survey reports on work patterns and preferences of American workers.

U.S. Department of Labor, Women's Bureau. 1984. 20 facts on women workers.

———. 1985. Earnings difference between women and men workers. Fact sheet no. 85-7.

———. 1985. Black women in the labor force. Fact sheet no. 85-6.

———. 1985. Working age disabled women. Fact sheet no. 85-3.

———. 1985. Federal job training and vocational education legislation that benefits women. Fact sheet no. 85-10.

———. 1985. The retirement equity act of 1984. Fact sheet no. 85-8.

———. 1985. Advances for women through federal legislation during the United Nations decade for women, 1976-1985. Fact sheet no. 85-9.

———. 1986. Women who maintain families. Fact sheet no. 86-2.

Vanek, J. 1974. Time spent in housework. *Scientific American* 231: 116-20.

Vicker, R. 4 August 1983. To work at home instead of commuting. *Wall Street Journal.*

Walker, K. E. 1970. Time spent by husbands in household work. *Family Economics Review* 4: 8-11.

Webb, M. December 1983. Life in the electronic cottage. *Working Woman.*

Weigand, R. E. 19 April 1986. What's a fair day's work? *New York Times.*

Werneke, D. 1983. *Microelectronics and office jobs: The impact of the chip on women's employment.* Geneva: International Labour Office.

Wessel, D. 22 September 1986. Growing gap: U.S. rich and poor increase in numbers; middle loses ground. *Wall Street Journal.*

Wolfgram, T. 1984. Working at home. *Futurist* 18: 31-34.

Index